BENEFITS

INVESTING IN THE FUTURE

JOAN BROWN

CPAG Ltd
1–5 Bath Street,
London EC1V 9PY
June 1988

© CPAG Limited 1988
ISBN 0 946744 11 4

The views expressed in this book are not necessarily those of the Child Poverty Action Group

Cover design by Calvert's Press
Typeset by Nancy White
Printed by Calvert's Press, 31-39 Redchurch Street, London E2

Contents

Acknowledgements	iv
Note on the author	v
Introduction *Fran Bennett*	vii
Update	xv
1 Do we value our children?	1
2 Child benefit and low income families	7
3 Child benefit, tax and the family	28
4 Child benefit for all families — sharing the cost of children	35
5 The protection of children	45
6 Changing the nature of child benefit — the consequences	55
7 Allocating resources wisely	62

Acknowledgements

Thanks are due to Fran Bennett, Peter Golding and Peter Townsend for their helpful readers' comments; and to Sue Lind and Julia Lewis at CPAG for their help with the production of this book. I am especially grateful to the staff at the House of Commons Library for all their time spent aiding my research work.

Note on the author

Joan Brown is a self-employed researcher and writer on social policy. She is also the author of many books on social security, including: *Children in Social Security; Family Income Supplement; The Future of Family Income Support* (published by the Policy Studies Institute); and, most recently, *In Search of a Policy: the Rationale for Social Security Provision for One-Parent Families* (published by the National Council for One Parent Families).

Introduction

> For the sake of our country's future, the needs of children must come first.
>
> Mother of 3, *Mother's Life-line*, 1985

CPAG has always been involved in debates about ways in which help is provided for families with children. And, since its introduction in the late 1970s, child benefit has been one of our main concerns. As an anti-poverty group, we have supported it because, for poor families on means-tested benefits, it provides a regular and reliable source of income which is not affected by changes in their marital or employment status or their other income; indeed, those organisations with the greatest practical experience of working closely with poor families are amongst the most enthusiastic supporters of universal child benefit. We also know from experience that child benefit reaches all those low income families that benefits specifically designed for the poor often don't reach: the seemingly intractable 'take-up problems' of means-tested benefits do not affect child benefit. Unlike those benefits which are reserved for the poor alone, child benefit is popular with those who receive it. In addition, we have supported child benefit because, being paid to the main carer (usually the mother), it is more likely to be spent on the children's needs.

In common with many other organisations representing families, women and children, we have also supported child benefit because, as a benefit paid to all families, it is concrete evidence of the value attached to children and child-rearing by society. It helps to transfer resources over the family life-cycle, to the point at which needs are greater and income often lower. As the replacement for the old child tax allowance (and family allowances), it is an attempt to equalise the tax burden between those with and those without children. And it represents an investment in the next generation by the community as a whole.

So far, so good. But why should CPAG ask Joan Brown — an author already well-known for her writing on social security in general and family benefits in particular — to look again at the case for child benefit in a new pamphlet at this particular time?

First, because it is being suggested by some people that universal child benefit is now outdated and has outlived its usefulness. The argument is that, as the economy grows and more people become better off, some (or most) do not 'need' child benefit: they can well afford to bring up their children without assistance, and should do so, since it was their choice to have them in the first place. The tax cuts in recent Budgets have given them additional resources; and women's equality has progressed so far that mothers no longer 'need' child benefit as an independent source of income. *The* concept recommended by the government for the benefits system for the remainder of the century is 'targeting'. The new benefits introduced from April 1988, especially income support (with its family premium) and family credit (with its more generous amounts for low paid families) are 'targeted' on those low income families who need help. As child benefit is not 'targeted' (ie, means-tested), its continued payment in its present form is said to be inappropriate — or at least should be seriously questioned.

CPAG therefore believed that the time was ripe to examine the case for child benefit for the 1990s — to explore whether the current criticisms are correct, or whether, on the contrary, there is a valid viewpoint that child benefit is *more* vital now than ever before, given changing patterns of family formation and labour market conditions.

Secondly, and more specifically, since the autumn of 1987 there have been persistent press rumours that an internal government review of child benefit is under way. By the spring of 1988, press reports were suggesting that the major objective of such a review was *not* to examine possible improvements or increases in child benefit, but to limit the amount spent on it — and that the options under consideration included taxing or means-testing child benefit, or merging it with the new family credit scheme (in effect, abolishing it altogether). A decision was said to be expected in the coming round of public expenditure discussions in the summer or autumn of 1988.

These press reports gave a further, and more urgent, impetus to CPAG's decision to publish a pamphlet which would examine, in a careful and considered way, the current debate around the future of child benefit and the functions· which it performs for families at different income levels and for the community as a whole.

Until quite recently, there would have been no question of the current child benefit arrangements being discontinued. The government's Green Paper, which followed the 'comprehensive' social security reviews of 1984/85, endorsed the principles underlying the universal child benefit scheme:

> The government accept the case for continuing the system of child benefit. It is right that families with children at all income levels should receive some recognition for the additional costs of bringing up children and that the tax/benefit system should

allow for some general redistribution of resources from those without children to those who have the responsibility of caring for them.

Green Paper, *Reform of Social Security*, Vol 2, p 48

And it continued: 'the case for changing [child benefit] has not been made out. The government do not therefore propose to alter its basis or structure.'

This explicit conclusion was echoed in the Conservative Party's manifesto for the 1987 election, which promised that 'child benefit will continue to be paid as now, and direct to the mother'. Moreover, both before and after the election, ministers spelt out what this commitment meant in greater detail:

...I can tell you that child benefit will continue as a non-means-tested universal payment, paid to the mother and tax-free. There ought to be no question about that.

Rt Hon John Major MP, then Minister for Social Security, interviewed by Richard Berthoud, *Poverty 66*, Spring 1987

...The words say that [child] benefit would be paid as a universal benefit, tax-free, and to the mother... I believe that that obligation was right.

Nicholas Scott MP, Minister for Social Security, January 1988

Ministers were always careful, of course, to add that the government's commitment to the *form* of child benefit implied no guarantee about its *level*. There was no commitment that child benefit would be uprated every year in line with inflation. Indeed, the Green Paper of 1985 had already made clear that the government wished to see priority given to the new means-tested benefits for families with children, introduced in April 1988. In that month, child benefit was frozen for at least a year, and ministers constantly emphasised the 'additional' £320m which they claimed to be spending on low income families, compared with the £120m 'saved' by not uprating child benefit.

CPAG — and the many other groups representing the interests of women, families and children, who make up the Save Child Benefit coalition — thus saw their fears beginning to be realised: child benefit might be allowed to 'wither away', through reductions in its real value, until a government could claim that it was no longer worth retaining.

This had always been the implication in the longer term of the Green Paper's explicit declaration that, 'although the general principle of providing support to families through child benefit is important, the greatest priority for additional resources in the area of family support is to provide better targeted help for those on low incomes'. (*Reform of Social Security*, Vol 2, p 48). However, in the various debates on the planned freeze in child benefit which took place in parliament between the autumn of 1987 and the spring of 1988, Conservative MPs challenged the government's apparent view that resources for improving benefits for poor families had to be found by reductions in the benefit received by all families:

> ...what we want to do is to target money to the poorest families. Conservative Members are all very much in favour of that, but... why are we taking it from other families, rather than from the general taxpayer?
>
> Tony Marlow MP, November 1987

This argument gained added weight when set against the reductions in taxation for 'the general taxpayer' made in the 1988 Budget.

The government's Green Paper of 1985 had, however, been emphatic about the 'two clear and distinct aims in helping families with the costs of children' and about the dangers of confusing them:

> The first is to provide help for families generally while the second is to provide extra help for low income families. It would be a serious mistake to confuse these two purposes or to seek to restructure a benefit designed to meet one aim in order to meet the other aim.
>
> *Reform of Social Security*, Vol 2, p 48

But the government now seems to be tempted to do exactly that. It appears to be contemplating ways to 'restructure' child benefit by reducing it for or withdrawing it entirely from many families, contrary to its own advice given in the Green Paper.

This would be a more drastic step than the slow process of attrition feared by child benefit's many supporters. Recent statements and letters from ministers have increasingly been emphasising the 'cost' and 'ill-targeted nature' of child benefit, and suggesting that it is right to keep it 'under continual review in order to assess its cost-effectiveness and relevance to the needs of today's society'. And, despite the Conservative Party's statements, when in opposition, that increases in child benefit would be seen as part of its strategy of cuts in taxation, references to child benefit's function as the equivalent of a tax allowance for families with children have been notable by their absence from ministerial speeches and letters recently. Fears are growing for the future of child benefit in its present form.

At the time of publication of this pamphlet, those fears have not yet been dispelled. Whether the future of child benefit is under threat from a year-on-year process of reductions in its real value, culminating in possible abolition (as happened with the maternity grant recently), or whether a more drastic short cut of taxation, means-testing or abolition is planned in the shorter term, CPAG hopes that this pamphlet will remind readers of the many advantages of a benefit paid to *all* families to help meet their children's needs.

The pamphlet is not just a reminder of arguments which remain as valid as they have always been over the past decade, however. Joan Brown argues in addition that there are compelling reasons for rejecting John Moore's (the Secretary of State's) view that those who defend a universal child benefit are unable to 'get out of the past'. On the contrary, child benefit can be seen as *the* benefit of the future.

It is flexible enough to cope with instability in family relationships, and provides some security and stability to children and their parents in the changing labour market of the late twentieth century, with its growing proportion of part-time and temporary jobs and the hazards of increasing self-employment.

Because it is not withdrawn as other income rises, child benefit also fulfils the Secretary of State's own criterion for 'welfare measures ... to *really* promote economic and social welfare' which, he says, 'must be aimed ultimately at encouraging independence, not dependence': child benefit provides a floor for families to build on by their own efforts, rather than a ceiling trapping them into long-term poverty or near poverty. If 'the next step forward in the long evolutionary march of the welfare state in Britain is away from dependence towards independence', as John Moore said in his speech of 26 September 1987, child benefit is a crucial part of that next step forward.

The government is currently urging us all to look forward to 1992, when the single European market comes into operation. Perhaps we should also take the opportunity to look at the social policies of our European neighbours to see what we can learn from them. CPAG believes that two important lessons emerge.

First, although some European governments, when economic difficulties were at their height, sought ways to control the cost of child benefits, all of them have thought it right to maintain a benefit for children which is not restricted to poor families. At a time when we are drawing ever closer to Europe in our commercial and trading activities, and when the harmonisation of social security benefits is under examination as a longer-term goal of the European Community, do we really want to step backwards and so far out of line?

Secondly, many European countries also recognise that there are a variety of other ways in which parental responsibilities and the care of children can be positively encouraged. CPAG has never argued that child benefit can stand alone as the only means of preventing poverty amongst families with children. Measures such as increased provision of child-care facilities, better social security benefits for part-time workers, improved maternity benefits, pay and leave, and parental and family leave, would have a marked impact on women's employment opportunities and incomes — and hence, we believe, on the particular difficulties faced by families with children. In some of these areas, too, many of our European neighbours are now more forward-looking and generous than we seem to be prepared to be in this country.

CPAG would welcome the opportunity to contribute to debates about improved provision in these areas — and, indeed, about ways of improving the 'targeting' of child benefit which would not compromise its other valuable functions, described by Joan Brown in this pamphlet.

But we have not been asked to contribute to such a forward-looking debate. Instead, it appears that the government is conducting its own review of child benefit, in secret, which may be considering reneging on its manifesto commitment and recent ministerial statements. It is the government's review, not child benefit's supporters, which seems unable to 'get out of the past'. It appears that child benefit is a prime target for possible cuts merely because it represents a large item of public expenditure; yet it seems illogical to allow such important decisions to be determined by the Treasury's outdated accounting methods, which do not treat the equally large amounts spent on tax allowances and reliefs as public expenditure, because they represent revenue foregone rather than revenue spent. It also seems particularly perverse to be thinking of cutting spending on child benefit at a time when the economy is said to be in a very healthy state and generous tax cuts are demonstrably affordable.

Michael Portillo MP, Social Security Minister, claimed recently on behalf of the government that 'we give vigorous moral support to the family' (*Hansard*, 12 November 1987). It seems to us, however, that there is something rather morally dubious in the growing trend described by Joan Brown in the first chapter of this pamphlet to see children as just another kind of consumer good, chosen by their parents in preference to a better house, a foreign holiday or a yacht. A government which aims to give 'vigorous moral support' to the family should be vigorously challenging such a view. The continued payment of child benefit to all families provides one means of expression for the contrary view — that children are not privately-owned consumer durables but represent the future for us all.

As long ago as 1972, Margaret Wynn wrote: 'If the objective of social policy is restricted to the elimination of poverty, it is unlikely to succeed because it must isolate the poor and fail to win the support of the majority of families' (*Family Policy*, Penguin, 1972). Her judgement is supported by those who have, more recently, examined the current composition of social security policies across various Western countries and their potential in the future: 'Universal benefits contribute to a nation's sense of community and interdependence — to national solidarity' (*Into the 21st Century*, International Labour Office, 1984).

CPAG hopes that this pamphlet will persuade its readers — including, we hope, MPs and ministers — that the government should not be asking how much can be 'saved' from child benefit, but how this valuable multi-purpose benefit can be maintained and improved as an investment in the future into the twenty-first century.

Fran Bennett
Director, CPAG

Update

Just as we went to press, the Prime Minister stated in the House of Commons:

> I agree with the Hon Gentleman that the [1987 Conservative] manifesto clearly stated: 'Child benefit will continue to be paid as now, and direct to the mother.' That commitment will be honoured.
>
> (Oral answer to John Cartwright MP, 17 May 1988)

As explained in the Introduction, one of the reasons why CPAG commissioned Joan Brown to write this pamphlet was the existence of persistent rumours that an internal government review of child benefit was under way, examining such possibilities as means-testing or taxing child benefit. Suspicions were confirmed when Nicholas Scott MP, Minister for Social Security, refused to assure MPs (in mid-March 1988) that the manifesto commitment would not be diluted within the lifetime of this parliament.

Given the Prime Minister's well-founded reputation for not 'turning', her personal reiteration of the manifesto pledge seems to suggest that the *form* of child benefit will not be changed (for example, by means-testing or taxing it) this side of the next election. If this interpretation is correct, CPAG would, of course, be delighted — and relieved.

However, press comment at the time of the Prime Minister's statement did *not* indicate that the review had immediately been called off — merely that the government might be planning to proceed with more caution, perhaps producing a Green Paper during this parliament with proposals for action in the next. And in the meantime, the press reports also suggested, the constant (and growing) threat to the *level* of child benefit continued — with the real possibility of a further freeze in its level in 1989, and perhaps beyond. The maternity and death grants 'withered away' in just such a manner, prior to their abolition last year.

We take heart, therefore, from the sensitivity being shown by the government to the concern expressed by its own backbench MPs (amongst many others) about the future of child benefit. But we continue to be seriously concerned about the real value of child benefit in the short term, and about the threat to its continuation in its present form in the longer term. We hope that this pamphlet will lead to a more informed debate on these issues, not only amongst those who are already convinced supporters of child benefit, but also amongst a wider audience.

Fran Bennett
Director, CPAG   June 1988

1 Do we value our children?

In recent years, there has been a tendency to see children as just one more kind of consumer choice. The line of argument is that, while some people's preference is for a comfortable home equipped with all the modern devices, holidays in distant places, an active social life and a new model car or two, others choose instead to have children as their preferred source of pleasure and satisfaction. Since the child is just a different sort of consumer durable, then to subsidise children in any way is no more justifiable than subsidising the purchase of a new washing machine, or a home computer, or a boat.

Such an approach, if pressed to its logical conclusion, would of course imply that children warrant no more consideration than other goods. Like other consumer durables, they might be treasured and cared for but could also be disposed of when no longer wanted, or exploited to produce extra pleasure. This attitude devalues children — who are human beings with their own human rights — and, if this attitude were adopted as a basis for policy, it would debase the society which accepted it.

Having children is a private matter...

Just the same, it is true that, for most people, having children is a conscious choice, and one which they believe will bring them fulfilment and happiness. While some decisions to adopt or foster a child may be partly altruistic, for most people the choice to have a child is made for complex personal reasons. Would-be parents do not set out to populate the country or to provide its future workforce or defence forces. Having children is, to use Michael Beenstock's phrase, 'essentially a private matter'.

Beenstock goes on to argue that 'if parents choose to procreate and are in a position to care properly for their offspring, no matters of public interest or concern arise'.[1] Similarly, the Institute for Fiscal Studies (IFS) comments that parents choose to have children 'for reasons of personal pleasure rather than social obligation' and asks 'what then is the source of the claim on the rest of society?'[2] In this view, the state may have a duty to protect children from harm (including any harm arising from the poverty of their parents); but otherwise a public interest in children does not arise.

...but a public concern

But a nation *cannot* be wholly indifferent to the choice its people make about having children. Children are its future. Indeed, in some countries (France, for example), the fear of having too few children leads to active government policies — usually described as pro-natalist — to encourage a higher birth rate. In this country, apart from a mild panic about a falling birth rate in the 1930s, it has not been seen as the government's business to provide financial incentives for child-bearing, and few would wish to change this.

Population projections for future British birth rates (fertility) suggest that no marked changes are likely. But the Office of Population Censuses and Surveys (OPCS) does point out that:

> Changing attitudes to marriage and child-bearing, in particular a trend towards an increasing proportion of childless women in the population, are features of the current scene which many commentators consider likely to persist...[3]

In West Germany, as many as twenty per cent of women are choosing not to have any children at all.[4] Figures from the OPCS suggest that the UK is heading in the same direction.[5]

The influences that lead people to make their choices are not always easy to discern. Some infertile couples are almost desperate to have children, while others, well able to have children, choose not to do so. Certainly there are economic and social pressures — the cost of housing and insecurity of employment on the one hand, and the desire of women to pursue a career on the other — which can lead to the postponement of child-bearing, or a decision to have a small family, or perhaps to avoid having children altogether.

Child benefit was paid for:
  13,595,000 children in 1978
  12,346,000 children in 1985

Child benefit was paid to:
  7,135,000 families in 1978
  6,819,000 families in 1985

('Social Security Statistics — Great Britain', 1982 and 1986, HMSO, London)

Fig 1 — How many children? How many families?

It is right that we should be sceptical about the usefulness of pro-natalist policies, but current trends suggest that governments should be cautious about adopting policies which penalise families in economic terms more than is already the case. It is one thing to decide not to offer people active encouragement to have children. It is quite another to weight the choice *against* children. One report from the Committee on Social Affairs and Employment (European Parliament), entitled 'A Community Family Policy', included the following statement:

> Respect for the right of individuals to make their own decisions with regard to their family life, their fertility and the founding of a family must continue to be the rule... However, Europe must encourage the provision of resources to make families' choices easier, to increase their freedom and to allow family plans to be carried out.

Our own self-interest...

Whether we have more or fewer children, there are plenty of good reasons why there should be a public interest in their well-being, which apply whether or not we have children ourselves.

Each year, around 720,000 children are born in the UK, and everyone in the country has a vested interest in them. Whether these children grow up with a sense of belonging to a country which cares about them, or feel alienated from a society which seemed indifferent to them in their childhood, matters to each one of us — because we will reap the benefit or pay the price accordingly. Equally, whether they are fit or unhealthy, educated up to their capacity or ill-equipped for the future, law-abiding or criminal, will affect us as well as them. It is these children, as adults, who will make choices and decisions which will influence our well-being, and who will support the services — such as the National Health Service, pensions, refuse collection or national defence — which will be needed at some time or other by all citizens.

The responsibility for child-rearing is placed with parents. However, while society cannot bring up children, it can, through its institutions and resources, choose to support the parental role. Self-interest dictates that it should find the appropriate means of doing so. As the National Children's Bureau wrote, in evidence to the *Social Security Review*, in 1984:

> Children constitute our future. The contributions of all taxpayers are used to build roads, schools and railway lines. By the same token, they should contribute towards the human capital that constitutes the future of our nation.

...but not only self-interest

Self-interest is a good practical guide; but it should also be a matter of national pride that we protect the rights and interests of our youngest citizens in their most vulnerable years.

The minimum we should expect are laws to enable the state to intervene if parents fail badly to meet their responsibilities, and to punish them if this seems necessary. But we should surely aim to do more than this. We should seek to ensure for our children as good a start in life as we can. For this purpose, we need positive policies to help parents to carry out their vital task of bringing up the nation's children.

A policy for the family

A 'policy for the family' can have many aspects. Families with children can be — and are — assisted through the health services, the provision of education, housing policies, access to employment, through tax provisions and, finally, through social security arrangements. The ordinary citizen wants in particular to see a high standard of provision for all children in our health and education services, and an end to homelessness and bad housing conditions, especially for families with children. In the run-up to the 1988 Budget there was plenty of evidence that public expenditure on these services for families is not begrudged by the average taxpayer.

This pamphlet is about one facet of family policy — child benefit — but it has to be seen in the context of the full range of policies and it must be judged on the same terms as the other policies. There is often a tendency to speak of social security (and, rightly or wrongly, child benefit is placed within this category) as if it were a thing apart, subject to quite different considerations from other elements of policy. In some respects this may be correct; when thinking about child benefit, it is important to remember that different policy considerations ought only to be applied where genuine and justifiable differences exist.

Child benefit — a flexible mechanism

Child benefit is a family income support mechanism with multiple functions:

- ☐ It reduces poverty among families with children.
- ☐ It removes a possible disincentive to work which could arise if children in families on social security were treated much more favourably than children from low income working families, and therefore helps the labour market to function better.
- ☐ It acts as a form of tax relief, ensuring fairness in the taxation of those with and without children.
- ☐ It serves the general community interest in the well-being of children by sharing with families the high cost of child-rearing.

☐ It helps to support young people who remain in full-time education after 16 years and recently has been given a part to play in supporting new school leavers, those awaiting entry to training and those who have a job to go to but await the starting date.

With the exception of the role of supporting those who have left the education system, these were the tasks given to family allowances from 1945, together with the much older child tax allowance. The latter first appeared in the period 1798 to 1805 and was reintroduced in 1909. These roles were reinforced by the introduction of child benefit, which integrated family allowances and child tax allowances as from 1977.

But what is the future of child benefit?

The wide range of functions which child benefit performs has attracted equally wide-ranging support for this benefit. This support — from the political right as well as the centre and the left, from business as well as unions, from organisations concerned with the average family as well as those focused on the needs of the poorest families, from teachers, social workers and academics, from women's organisations and consumers' representatives, and many others — was well in evidence in the 1984/85 Social Security Review which subjected the benefit to intense scrutiny.

Yet child benefit is now under attack — led by the government — which means that it is no longer possible to assume that this benefit, however highly thought of, is safe. It is being argued that, if there is a desire to combat poverty while maintaining work incentives, this is better and cheaper if done through means-tested benefits than through universal child benefit. Chapter 2 Parts I and II examine this assertion. (It should be noted that the term 'work' used throughout this text refers to *paid* employment as opposed to housework and child-rearing which is usually unpaid.)

It seems that the government now prefers to ignore the fact that child benefit replaced the old child tax allowance and that it has a function in relation to the taxation of families. Chapter 3 looks at the case for maintaining child benefit as a child tax credit and the questions raised by paying child benefit to the rich.

There is now a strong tendency to question the desirability of paying child benefit to the ordinary family, on the grounds that it is no longer necessary for the community to share in the cost of bringing up children, since the family can add to its own income through the paid employment of the mother. Chapter 4 examines the position of the modern family and the realities of women's employment patterns.

Chapter 5 introduces an element not usually addressed by opponents of child benefit. The 1980s are a period of greater insecurity for children, brought about by family change, labour market changes, the growth of one-parent families and (an older problem) the way income is distributed within families. This chapter argues that child benefit is now performing an important child protection function.

The government is examining ways in which the cost of child benefit can be reduced. Chapter 6 sets out the consequences for families of moves to abolish, freeze or cut child benefit.

Finally, the government frequently claims that child benefit is too costly and that increases in the benefit cannot be afforded. Chapter 7 considers the validity of these statements.

Notes

1. Michael Beenstock, 'Rationalising Child Benefit', paper given to a PSI seminar in June 1984.
2. A W Dilnot, J A Kay and C N Morris, *The Reform of Social Security*, IFS/Clarendon Press, Oxford, 1984.
3. OPCS Monitor PP2/86/1.
4. Jean-Claude Chenais, 'Population Trends in the European Economic Community 1960-1987', paper given to the Conference on Demographic Change and its Socio-Economic Consequences, Centre for European Policy Studies, Belgium, 1987.
5. Barry Werner, 'Family Building Intentions of Different Generations of Women: Results from the General Household Survey 1979-83', *Population Trends*, Summer 1986.

2 Child benefit and low-income families

PART I: CHILD POVERTY AND WORK INCENTIVES

Two of child benefit's multiple functions promote objectives that command a wide range of support — the ending of child poverty and the maintenance of work incentives.

In the past, many thought that you had to choose between these two goals. Many children had to be poor in order to ensure that their parents had an incentive to work. The root of the problem was then, and is still, that the wages paid for a job were set according to the requirements of that job and to market demand. The rate for the job would be paid whether the worker was married or single, with or without children. If the wage was too low to support the family, the children would be in poverty. That was how the market worked — and works today.

In contrast, social security benefits have always been allocated largely according to need, albeit at a minimum level. This is especially so in the case of means-tested benefits such as the old Poor Law and the current income support scheme (previously supplementary benefit). This implied that there was a basic rate for an individual or a couple, with additions for each child. The difficulty then was that, if the benefits were set at a reasonable minimum which kept the family out of poverty, the unemployed family man who was offered low paid work could find that his benefits were as high as his prospective wages and would have no obvious incentive to go back to work.

The answer the Poor Law found for this (in 1834) was the principle of 'less eligibility'. In other words, benefits had to be set lower than the lowest wages in order to maintain work incentives. It followed that if the children of workers were poor, the children of the unemployed had to be even poorer, and not only the children of the unemployed, but all other children whose families were on benefit such as the sick and disabled who were unable to work.

The old remedy not forgotten

As long as there are substantial numbers of low paid jobs which unemployed people might be expected to fill, the issue of the effect of benefit levels on work incentives will not go away. It has now acquired the popular name of the unemployment trap. Using a widely agreed definition of low pay as being below two-thirds of the median male wage gives a figure of £123 (gross) per week in 1986/7. The figures in Fig 2 show the numbers of people who earned less (and often much less) than £123 per week, and those who earned less than the equivalent hourly rate in part-time work. They show that there is a very large sector of the labour force who are low paid. Although not all the people in low paid jobs are poor (for example, they may be single and living with their parents or married women with a working husband), it is the wages paid by these jobs which are compared with the social security benefits for people with children.

The old remedy for ensuring that there was a gap between benefits and low wages, to improve work incentives, has not been forgotten. The Institute of Directors, for example, in its evidence to the Social Security Review 1984/85,[1] placed much emphasis on strengthening the incentive to take low paid work. Its plan was to restore the old Poor Law principle of 'less eligibility'. The Institute argued that the 'fundamental' problem was that supplementary benefit rates for both adults and children were too high in relation to low wages. Benefit rates, including the rates for children, should therefore be cut. While the purpose of the social security system should be the relief of poverty, this must be 'subject to the less eligibility principle'.

Full-time workers, including overtime:
   20% of male manual workers
   9.5% of male non-manual workers
   73% of female manual workers
   43% of female non-manual workers
Total men who are low paid — 1.59 million
Total women who are low paid — 2.57 million

Part-time male and female workers on low hourly rates:
   80% of women — 3.18 million
   73% of men — 600,000

(Robin Smail, 'Low Pay in Britain — The Latest Survey', *Low Pay Review*, Spring 1987)

Fig 2 — On low pay (£123/week or below) in Great Britain in 1986/87

This 'remedy' ignored some important facts. First, there are many poor low paid workers with children. On the government's own figures for 1983 there were 940,000 working families in the low income band, including 110,000 with incomes below supplementary benefit level. In all, these families had 1.6 million children.[2] They are witness to the failure to tackle effectively the poverty and near poverty of children in working families, but they are certainly not evidence of lack of work incentive. On the contrary, these parents have taken low paid jobs even though they offer much the same low standard of living as life on benefits. The figures emphasise the fact that the unemployment trap — that is, the lack of cash incentive to get back to work — is in many ways a theoretical issue. In practical terms, people do want to work and prefer even low earnings to dependence on benefits.[3] Second, the old remedy reapplied would not only leave the children of low paid workers in poverty, but would significantly increase poverty among the children of the unemployed and other benefit recipients.

The search for a better remedy

For over half a century, it has been argued — and is now usually accepted — that if you want to tackle child poverty in families on social security benefits and in families on low pay, and at the same time maintain work incentives, the answer is *not* to reduce the level of social security for those out of work but to increase the income of low paid workers. Since the alternative mechanism of a minimum wage has been rejected by governments for all this time (except for the minimal Wages Council provisions), and since the problem arose even in the period when low paid workers paid no tax, the attempt to tackle child poverty has had to be made through social security benefits of one sort or another.

There were two approaches. The first was to try to neutralise the effect of children on the move between unemployment and work by paying a benefit for all children. This could at the same time protect the children of all those on benefit, including the children of the unemployed, and tackle poverty among the children of low paid workers. This was the family allowance/child benefit remedy.

The second was to pay means-tested benefits to low paid workers, either as a direct supplement to wages or as a means of reducing their essential costs. This was the family income supplement and housing benefit remedy.

Unfortunately, governments applied neither remedy properly, principally because it clashed with another of their objectives — to limit public expenditure on benefits. Child benefit was too low. The help with housing costs offered to low paid workers was less than that given to those on social security benefits, and family income supplement was set at a low level and did not take proper account of the cost of children. So the problem of child poverty and worries about work incentives — the unemployment trap — persisted. But, in addition to this, the use of means-tested benefits for wage-earners created a third problem — the poverty trap — and brought to the fore a fourth problem — take-up.

Children in low income families

The figures given in Fig 3 show, without any doubt, that child poverty has persisted and that large numbers of children (thirty-one per cent of all children) are living in low to very low income families. Indeed, it is a dismal but clear picture of our failure as a nation to protect children against poverty and low living standards and to offer them a good start in life.

☐ In 1983, **400,000 children** lived in families with incomes below supplementary benefit level. These included both working and non-working families.

☐ In 1983, **1.6 million children** were living on supplementary benefit. By 1987, this had risen to **2.24 million children** on supplementary benefit.

☐ In 1983, **3.8 million children or 31% of all children** lived in low income families. These had incomes below, on, or up to 40% above, the supplementary level. Together they make up **27% of all families**.

☐ In 1982, 58% of couples with children living on supplementary benefit ran out of money most weeks, 70% had experienced a period of acute anxiety about money problems while on benefit, 63% lacked a complete standard set of clothing, and 56% were in debt when they were interviewed.

☐ In 1985, the government defined the level of income of families 'with the greatest needs' as the bottom 20% of the national distribution of income, with family income adjusted for family size. It found that (in 1982) **18% of all working age couples with children and 41% of one-parent families** were living at this very low level.

(Social Security Statistics, 1986, HMSO, London; *Hansard*, 30 June 1987, col 68; Richard Berthoud, *Reform of Supplementary Benefit*, PSI, 1985; and Green Paper, 'Reform of Social Security', Cmnd 9519, HMSO, 1985)

Fig 3 — Children and poverty

Britain has no official poverty line and in the 1985 Green Paper on the reform of social security the government refused to discuss the subject.[4] Up to now it has been necessary to make do with measuring income in relation to the supplementary benefit level. For years groups concerned about the family (including CPAG) have argued that these benefit levels were too low and that families on supplementary benefit should be counted as being in poverty, while those up to forty per cent above should be classified as being 'on the margins of poverty'.

In the Social Security Review 1984/85, the government had to agree that supplementary benefit for families with children *was* too low, and so was the equivalent level of income for those in low paid jobs, even after their benefits had been added. What is more, the number of families who had severe problems in making ends meet had increased over the previous decade. This was clearly evidenced in the Green Paper, *Reform of Social Security:*

> In the 1930s, working age families were seen as the main group in poverty... By the 1950s and 1960s, pensioners were the major cause for concern. Now the position has changed again and in 1985, it is families with children who face the most difficult problems.[5]

> Families containing dependent children now account for over half of all individuals living on low incomes. This is an increase of nearly a fifth on the corresponding proportion ten years ago.[6]

But in future the government would measure poverty, not by comparing poor people with the rest of society, but by comparing them with one another. This is what is being done in Fig 4:

☐ 94% of families with 3 or more children where neither parent was employed;
☐ 75% of families with 1 or 2 children where neither parent was employed;
☐ 66% of non-working one-parent families;
☐ 60% of families with 1 or 2 children where the wife worked but the husband was unemployed;
☐ 58% of families with 3 or more children where the wife was in work but the husband was not;
☐ 31% of families with 3 or more children where the husband was in work but the wife was not;
☐ 15% of working one-parent families;
☐ 13% of families with 1 or 2 children where the husband but not the wife was in work.

Fig 4 — Families with children in the bottom 20% of national income[7]

Two definitions

At the time of the Social Security Review 1984/85 the problems of the 'poverty trap' and 'take-up' were giving rise to concern.

The poverty trap

The 'poverty trap' was the term used to describe the following situation. A low paid worker got an increase in wages, but for each £1 increase received, s/he had to pay more tax and more national insurance contributions while, at the same time, any means-tested benefits s/he was receiving would be reduced. In the process, most of the wage rise was swallowed up and, in some circumstances, the worker lost more than the actual wage increase. Deductions of this kind from an increase in wages are often described as the 'marginal tax rate'. For most people, in 1984, the tax and national insurance rate combined was thirty-nine per cent, but 210,000 families with children had a marginal tax rate of over seventy-five per cent when reduced benefits were taken into account[8] and sometimes the rate rose to over 100 per cent. These were higher marginal tax rates than those paid by the rich, and they mainly affected families with children.

There was also a secondary effect known as the 'poverty plateau'. If the worker only managed to keep around 7-10 pence of each £1 wage increase, the family's income hardly changed. Rather than getting a real boost from any wage increase, the family income moved upwards very slowly — and it could take many wage increases before the family finally reached a point where they no longer had to claim means-tested assistance. In all that time, the family's standard of living stayed at a very low level. Working lone mothers were also liable to spend long periods of time on the poverty plateau.

Part of the problem arose because the starting point for tax had fallen so low. There was a time in the 1950s when families at this low level of income paid no tax.[9] But the major factor responsible for increasing the number of families on low incomes was the use (some would say over-use) of means-tested benefits for earners — including not only family income supplement and housing benefit, but also free school meals or free milk, which could each be affected as the wage rose or when it passed a certain point.

Take-up

Take-up is the shorthand term for claiming ('taking up') benefits to which you are entitled. Benefits to which people see themselves as having a clear entitlement — because they are paid to everyone who has children (like child benefit) or because national insurance contributions have been paid for them (like pensions) — have an almost 100 per cent take-up rate. Means-tested benefits, however, have a much lower take-up rate, and the means-tested benefits available to those in work have the lowest rate of all, as Fig 5 shows:

Retirement pension	100%
Child benefit	100%
Supplementary benefit	83%
Housing benefit	77%
Family income supplement	54%
(*Social Trends*, 1987, HMSO, London)	

Fig 5 — Take-up, 1984, Great Britain

Low take-up of benefits had three effects. The benefits did not reach all the people who were entitled to them, and therefore failed in their objective to reduce poverty in a substantial proportion of cases. Low take-up of benefits for the low paid made the unemployment trap worse, since the benefits were designed to increase the gap between income for those in and out of work. But it did ease the poverty trap because, without some or all of the means-tested benefits, more of the wage increase stayed in the worker's pocket.

Which way ahead?

So the question which had to be faced then still faces us now in 1988: which is the best policy choice to tackle these problems? Is it the child benefit remedy or the means-tested solution — or perhaps a wise use of both methods in a well-balanced policy, bearing in mind both the needs of low income families and the other functions that child benefit has to perform for all families?

The government has decided to place a strong emphasis on the means-tested benefits and to downgrade the use of child benefit. The arguments it puts forward for this choice are summarised in the next section.

PART II: WHICH POLICY?

The government's case for emphasising the means-tested benefits

In making the case for emphasising means-testing, the government does state that it is desirable both to tackle child poverty and to increase work incentives; but it considers that to do this through higher child benefit would be far too costly, and even wasteful. Child benefit is paid to all families with children, regardless of income. It costs around £4.6 billion a year. Any increase in the benefit would flow through to all who are entitled to it, poor or not, and would cost an additional £40 million for each 10 pence increase.[10] An increase large enough to make an impact on poverty and work incentives would, it is said, be out of the question if public expenditure is to be kept under control — and that is one of the government's main priorities.

It is acknowledged that the rules and benefit rates applying to supplementary benefit, family income supplement and the 1982/83 housing benefit scheme produced very unsatisfactory results. But, the government argues, the new income support scheme, family credit and the revised housing benefit scheme offer considerable improvements and iron out most of the former problems.

Housing benefit is now paid on an equal basis to those in and out of work. It is true that, to achieve this, certain housing costs, such as water rates, are no longer directly covered for those not in work (but are, according to the government, being compensated for in the income support rates); and that the allowance made for mortgage interest has been halved for the first four months on income support. But this was considered necessary in order to be fair to low paid workers who did not receive help with these items. These changes, taken together, will reduce the unemployment trap, because they remove most of the effects caused by the rules for help with housing costs.

The new income support and family credit schemes are designed to offer a much better balance in the income available to those in and out of work, and will ensure that, for families with children, those working in low paid jobs will almost always get more income than those not in paid employment. This (in theory at least) means the virtual ending of the unemployment trap. As part of this process, it has been possible to give some increase in weekly benefits to unemployed families with children on income support as well as larger increases for many low paid families. Thus, the government claims, child poverty is being tackled.

By restricting the expenditure on child benefit (the argument goes on), more resources can be put into the means-tested schemes and so be directed to families in need, rather than being spread more thinly over all families, whether in need or not. In justification of its decision not to uprate child benefit for 1988/89 in line with inflation, the government pointed to the fact that more money was being allocated to income support and family credit.[11]

In the government's view, if child benefit were to be restricted further still, then the low income schemes could be further improved; if money were targeted on those who really need it, a real impact could be made on poverty. This might suggest to the government the need — in the longer term — to end the universal payment of child benefit, and this possibility has to be kept under review.

Many believe that restricting child benefit could go against the interests of those in need. But, it is argued, one way or another, child benefit is taken fully into account in setting the rates for children in both income support and family credit. This means that an increase in child benefit does not make any difference to the income of families on these benefits, since an equivalent amount will be deducted from their benefit rates. These families would therefore benefit more from improvements in the means-tested schemes.

The government acknowledges that the emphasis on means-tested benefits perpetuates the poverty trap. Efforts have been made to reduce the effects by assessing family credit and housing benefit on net income, rather than on gross income as in the old schemes. Free milk and free school meals have been withdrawn from low paid families and replaced with higher family credit. The total effect will be to ensure that it is not possible to lose the whole (or more) of a wage increase, as in the past; but it can still be the case that 80-95 pence in each extra £1 is lost. This is seen as regrettable, but not a sufficient reason to forgo the other advantages of a targeted approach.

Take-up is also recognised as a potential problem but, the government says, every effort will be made to secure a high take-up rate of family credit in particular. However, no guarantees can be offered on this point.

Taken overall, it makes quite a plausible case. But does it stand up to closer examination?

The case for greater emphasis on child benefit

The case for more emphasis on child benefit is, in part, the case against *over*-use of means-tested benefits, because of their defects. But it is also the case for the greater use of a more dynamic benefit — that is, a benefit which acts as a springboard to greater independence.

The deficiencies of means-testing

The nature of means-testing

Means-testing is for many people a demeaning process. It is necessary to prove that you are poor and, if in work, that you cannot earn enough to support and house your family. You must accept a substantial loss of privacy. Some of the information you give will be checked with your employer or your landlord. Further checks may be made on you at home. Your neighbours may be questioned. And, for some benefits, you must prove your eligibility again every six months, if you are to obtain the income which is essential to your family's well-being.

It is often suggested that an unnecessary fuss is made about this. After all, the whole population is means-tested through the tax system.

But there are significant differences. What is being assessed by the Inland Revenue is not the poverty of one part of the population to whom special rules are being applied. It is the ability of every adult to make an input into the collective funds to be spent on the public services.

Conflict with the tax authorities is most likely to arise out of a desire to minimise that input and, for most people, it is in the nature of a friendly joust. But conflict with the social security authorities about a means-tested benefit is, too often, a battle for survival. You cannot shrug your shoulders with a 'you win some, you lose some' attitude. The question facing you is how to feed the children next week.

On top of this, social security claimants, especially the unemployed and lone parents, have to learn to endure periodic campaigns in the media, by some members of parliament or by the government, against 'social security scroungers'. The majority who are honest claimants are tarred with the same brush as the small minority who claim benefits to which they are not entitled.

The contrast, then, between a non-means-tested benefit such as child benefit and a means-tested one, could hardly be greater. The government, in its Green Paper, *Reform of Social Security*, described child benefit as 'simple, well-understood and popular'.[12] A survey undertaken for the DHSS in 1985 on attitudes to the benefit found that 'child benefit has a fair, reasonable, wholesome image in most parents' eyes'.[13] In the words of one mother of three, living in the West Midlands:[14]

> The fact that it is not means-tested, but is given to everybody as a right...means there is no stigma attached to the money — as is the case with some benefits. Were it to be means-tested, many families most in need of it might not claim (as is the case with family income supplement).

Claiming the benefits
There is also a contrast in the claiming process for means-tested and non-means-tested benefits. Child benefit requires the simple proof that a child has been born to the family or has joined it. A small proportion of claims are more complex — for example, where the child spends part of the time in another home or has reached the age of 16 — but the vast majority are dealt with rapidly, following an uncomplicated postal claim.

Family credit can also be claimed by post, which is to the good. But if the experience of family income supplement is anything to go by, a claim will often involve lengthy correspondence. For the latter benefit, around seventy-five per cent of claims needed follow-up letters to clarify statements or obtain further information. The failure (or refusal) of employers to provide information on wages creates further long delays.[15] Many claims are settled quickly, but others can take months. Housing benefit requires a separate claim, this time to the local authority housing department, which also requires detailed and complicated information. The new claim form for income support is nineteen pages long and the speed with which a claim is settled will depend on how hard-pressed the local social security office is. For supplementary benefit some claims were settled quickly, while others were very much slower.

Family income supplement	23 days
Supplementary benefit	6 days
Child benefit	4 days

(*Hansard*, 12 January 1987, cols 105-6)

Fig 6 — Average interval between claim and initial payment in working days

Child benefit, once in payment, will be paid routinely to the parent or guardian until the child is 16 years old, as long as s/he is in his/her care. It has the notable characteristic of almost total reliability and regularity. Means-tested benefits, on the other hand, must be re-claimed at quite frequent intervals, when delays may recur. Problems may arise when there is a change of social security status — from unemployment to paid work or vice versa, or from being a two-parent family to becoming a one-parent family or vice versa. An allegation of fraud — 'I saw him working' or 'she has a man living there' — can lead to suspension of benefit while this is being investigated, even if the claimant proves, in the event, to be innocent. New benefit regulations can create administrative hold-ups — as in 1982/83 with the new housing benefit scheme, whose introduction was frankly chaotic.[16] During these periods of difficulty, child benefit is often the only benefit (and sometimes the only income) which continues in payment without complications or delays or humiliating enquiries.

Administration costs
The differences between the two types of benefit create costs for the taxpayer too. A straightforward benefit is much easier to administer, and costs proportionately less than the more complex benefits, as Fig 7 shows:

Supplementary benefit	8.5%
Family income supplement	4.5%
Child benefit	2.5%

(*Hansard*, 22 June 1984, cols 313-4)

Fig 7 — Administrative costs as a percentage of total costs

Take-up
All the above assumes that the low income family actually claims the benefit. But this is not always the case (see Fig 5). A poor rate of take-up is not an issue that can be dismissed lightly. The government's most optimistic forecast for the take-up of family credit is sixty per cent. (It sometimes uses the figure seventy per cent, but this refers to the proportion of the money available that will be claimed and not to the proportion of families claiming.) A sixty per cent take-up implies that forty per cent of eligible low income families will not receive family credit — the key benefit cited in the case for downgrading child benefit.

It is possible to take three attitudes to take-up. The first is that the only responsibility of government is to make these benefits available. If those who could claim them do not, that is their problem. The shop is open. If people do not come to 'buy', it is no fault of the shopkeeper. This view tends to ignore the fact that, normally, entering the average shop does not first involve confronting an obstacle course — much of which has been built by the shopkeeper — as claiming means-tested benefits does.

The second view is that take-up *is* a worrying problem, but that there *must* be an answer somewhere. John Major MP, when Minister of Social Security, said in an interview: 'We will try harder — I cannot conceive how we will not be able to push up the claim rate for family credit. I mean, I really cannot conceive it...the benefits are there for people to take up.'[17]

This approach represents the triumph of hope over experience. When family income supplement was introduced in parliament in 1970, the aim was to achieve an eighty-five per cent take-up rate. Sir Keith Joseph, the minister responsible at the time, indicated that he would do his best — and better — to achieve this, and said that the government 'intensely desire' a high take-up level.[18] This government, in particular, endeavoured to encourage a higher take-up rate of family income supplement, but with very limited success. In 1978-79, the rate was fifty-one per cent. It is now fifty-four per cent, although warnings are given with the official government statistics that it is more reliable to take the average take-up rate over a few years — ie, round about fifty per cent. The apparent increase to fifty-four per cent is said to be the result of improvements in the benefit rates which have encouraged more people to claim. The higher rate of family credit is expected to improve the situation a little more,[19] but even a sixty per cent rate seems somewhat optimistic in the light of past experience. There have been endless research studies into the problem of poor take-up rates. No solution has ever been found which does more than raise the rate by a couple of percentage points. It is doubtful if any effective solution exists — at least under the prevailing arrangements.

A third, rather different view, is that if child poverty is to be overcome, government has a responsibility, wherever feasible, to select benefit mechanisms which do not have take-up problems. At the least, it should not weight the provision on the side of benefits with bad take-up records, while downgrading a benefit which has an excellent record of take-up — child benefit. In the 1980s, around £57 million has gone unclaimed each year in family income supplement.[20] Unclaimed benefit does not figure as a problem in the child benefit scheme.

It is argued by some that both take-up problems and the stigma of means-tested benefits could be overcome by a radical restructuring of the tax and benefit system so that benefit rights were routinely assessed through the tax system.[21] Theoretically this is correct, but no scheme of this kind has ever been worked out in full, and it is not clear how well it could cope with changes in family circumstances and fluctuating incomes. There have to be doubts about this. In any case, no such option is before us. The new schemes are the old models reshaped, and although they are improved in some respects, there is no reason to believe that they will be free of the problems inherent in means-testing.

The unemployment trap
Because child benefit is not means-tested, when a family moves from unemployment to work the level of the benefit is not affected. This is the factor which has led to child benefit being seen as an important counter to the unemployment trap. This was an argument taken up by the Association of Independent Businesses in *Response to the Green Paper, 'Reform of Social Security'*:[22]

> The retention of child benefit is welcomed by the Association. We believe that child benefit is the pointer to the incentive to work issue and urge that the retention is allied to an increase in the child benefit rate in line with inflation. Increasing child benefit would not add to administrative costs and would have a favourable effect on wage restraint and would act as a stimulus to consumer demand.

To some extent, this function has now been taken over by the introduction of family credit, but child benefit is still important. For example, a family may be ignorant of its entitlement to family credit, or may experience difficulties with claiming it. If a family can *rely* on child benefit, it may make a positive choice *not* to rely on means-tested supplementation, opting for greater independence instead. (More will be said about this later.)

The poverty trap
It is accepted without argument that means-tested benefits which supplement low wages cannot fail to produce a poverty trap. This is so even in the radical schemes being put forward for paying means-tested benefits through the tax system. In its 1984 publication, *The Reform of Social Security* (Dilnot and others), the Institute for Fiscal Studies published the following statement:

> Do we need to 'institutionalise the poverty trap', as we expect our critics will observe? Can high marginal tax rates on the poor be avoided? We are forced, reluctantly, to conclude they cannot. We have seen no practical scheme that avoids this difficulty.

In its White Paper, *Reform of Social Security*,[23] the government itself admitted:

> Some...have pointed out that there is a price to be paid. In particular, the number of families facing high marginal tax rates but below 100 per cent will tend to increase. The government recognises this problem, which is unavoidable if available resources are to be directed towards those who need help most.

But one benefit does reduce the poverty trap — child benefit. It is not taxable; it is not included in the calculations for liability for national insurance contributions; it is not reduced as income rises. Weakening child benefit intensifies the impact of the poverty trap — increasing child benefit reduces this impact.

But does child benefit help the poor?

It is said that, because child benefit is taken into account in the setting of the rates for children in both income support and family credit, it no longer has an anti-poverty role to play. Whether child benefit gains or loses value makes no difference to the income received by recipients of these means-tested benefits. This is true, up to a point; but the whole argument needs closer inspection.

To begin with, it carries the assumption that there is no alternative policy. But this rule is not handed down in tablets of stone. It is government policy. Originally it was intended (by Beveridge) that the family allowance would be set at a rate sufficient to meet the minimum cost of a child and that, within social security, payment would be made only for the first child who was not eligible for the family allowance. This policy had to be abandoned because the rate of the family allowance was set too low and was rarely uprated. In order to protect children in families dependent on social security, a full social security rate was set for children (varying according to the adult benefit being paid) and this was paid partly as a child dependency addition (CDA) and partly as family allowance.

When child benefit was introduced, the practice was continued. It remained in force for supplementary benefit, has been implemented in the income support scheme and is now being applied to family credit. But the policy of protecting the child's social security income was abandoned after 1980 by the present government, if the family was drawing a national insurance benefit. This was done by changing the rules whereby a child's benefits were uprated, in such a way as to maintain the value of child benefit, while allowing the value of the CDA to go down.

By 1981, for the children of widows and disabled people, the value of the child's total benefit had already declined by thirteen per cent. At the time, the Social Security Advisory Committee (SSAC) criticised the practice,[24] but the decline has continued, though more slowly, since then. The impact on short-term benefits — such as unemployment and sickness benefit — was even more serious. Because their CDAs were already lower than those payable to the long-term claimants, the effect of the policy was to reduce the CDA to such a low level (15 pence) that, in 1984, the government was able to abolish it altogether. In future, the children of the unemployed and short-term sick would receive only child benefit.

More will be said about this later. But the point worth noting here is that, if the government can make these adverse changes to the policy which protected the child's social security benefits when decisions about child benefit were made, then *if it chose to do so*, it could equally make changes in the opposite direction. More specifically, the government could restore the goal of a benefit rate sufficient to meet the minimum cost of a child and adjust the formula which governs child benefit, in order to achieve this goal as quickly as possible.

Even if this policy change were not made, income support and family credit families would still regard it as important to maintain the value of child benefit, because it reduces their dependence on the more unreliable means-tested benefits. For families on family credit, child benefit can also help them to escape the poverty trap.

Child benefit — a key to independence

Because of the poverty trap and the poverty plateau, the means-tested benefits impede initiative and efforts made by the poor and near poor to change their circumstances. Means-tested benefits set a ceiling which holds down the family's standard of living, in spite of the family's hard work. Child benefit has quite a different effect. It acts as a foundation on which income can be built.

Child benefit has another important advantage. It frees many families from the need to claim means-tested benefits at all. This applies to working families who prefer to manage on their wages with the help of child benefit, rather than be subject to the many disadvantages of means-testing and the consequent loss of independence and self-reliance.

Again, child benefit is important to families not in work, because it gives them greater freedom to manage their limited income in a way that strengthens their independence and reduces dependency. The following quotations, respectively from the Association of Directors of Social Services,[25] from Frank Field MP,[26] and from the Minister for Social Security, Nicholas Scott,[27] all emphasise this point.

> An increased child benefit would help low wage families especially by providing a floor of income to build on. The family credit scheme shows that, however good the intentions, a means-tested benefit cannot meet the government's objective of providing income support without penalising the low paid for any wage increase by a punitive loss of benefits.

> But above all, child benefit has the fundamentally important role of increasing the freedom families experience in their everyday lives. Because child benefit is tax free, it acts as an income floor on which people can build by their own efforts.

> On the basis of benefit rates from April 1988 and expected claiming patterns, it is estimated that 500,000 families with 1 million dependent children would, but for child benefit, be entitled to income-related benefits.

The minister's boast is a proud one, and well worth making. But the figure could be even higher were it not for the government's own policies.

When the government reduced and then withdrew the CDA for the unemployed and sick (and lowered the value of the CDA for widows and disabled people), it pointed out, quite correctly, that any family in difficulty could claim supplementary benefit to make up their income to its former level. The same possibility applied in 1985, when child benefit was uprated by less than the rate of inflation, and in 1988 when it was frozen.

But the effect was that families who had previously managed on benefits for which they had contributed (and therefore claimed by right), with the help of the universal child benefit, were then faced with the choice of claiming means-tested benefits or going short. If they felt it necessary to claim, then their independence and their control over their own affairs were eroded. Conservative MP Sir Brandon Rhys Williams wrote a letter to *The Times* arguing this point:[28]

> If the real value of child benefit is now reduced, it will mean that even larger numbers of people will have to swallow their self-respect and apply to the DHSS for the wherewithal to keep their children above the minimum standard of nourishment and clothing to maintain their health and decency.

The total numbers of those affected are not easy to estimate, but as an example, the government believed that the effect of the 1988 child benefit freeze alone would be to draw 15,000 more families on to means-tested benefits.[29]

In contrast, an increase in child benefit would free thousands more families, both working and out of work, from the trap which means-tested benefits create. It would be a springboard to independence, a boost to effort and incentive, and, for many, a restoration of pride and self-respect.

Are means-tested benefits better for the poor?

It is seriously argued that there are good reasons that make the use of means-tested benefits preferable to the universal benefit, because this choice enables more resources to be concentrated on low income families. It is implied by the government that the savings from the latest freeze of child benefit — some £120 million — are being passed on to family credit and income support, together with £200 million more again.[30] But the government knew it would have to spend extra money anyway, to get its new schemes off the ground. And even if this were not so, can there be any confidence that improvements in a means-tested scheme will be maintained?

At a time when a new scheme or reform package is being implemented, any government tends to be reasonably generous in order to make the changes appear attractive. This is true of family credit, which is a considerable improvement on family income supplement in most respects, and will extend higher up the low income scale so that more low paid families will be entitled to claim. But, before becoming too optimistic about the future of the new scheme, it is instructive to consider the short history of housing benefit.

What happened to housing benefit?

After 1980, general housing subsidies to local authorities, which kept down the level of rents, were gradually withdrawn, on the grounds that they were poorly targeted and helped people who could afford higher rents. Rents were pushed up and, in 1982/83, a new, improved housing benefit scheme was introduced, which was intended to target help more towards low income families and to be fairer to those in *and* out of work.

This was to be a nil-cost reform; but within these limits, there were special transitional arrangements to help those who might lose from the change (as there are in 1988 for income support and family credit — and, as an afterthought, for housing benefit as well). And the tapers — the rate at which benefit is withdrawn as other income rises — were set quite low so as to permit some help quite far up the income scale, to help the 'near poor' as well as the poor.

When the bill came in, the government found that 6.9 million households (one in three of all households) were receiving benefit at a cost of £3.5 billion. The unexpectedly high numbers and costs were due to several factors. Inflation was one of these, but more important were the steep rise in rents and the large increase in unemployment which meant that many more people were in need. But, as a social security benefit, housing benefit was now regarded as far too costly and it was criticised because it helped people who were not strictly poor, but 'only' near poor.

Housing benefit was introduced in stages from November 1982 to April 1983. In November 1983, the first package of cuts was announced, and there have been further cuts each year since that time. These were achieved by ending the transitional arrangements, raising the tapers so as to withdraw benefit at a faster rate as income rose, increasing the amounts non-dependants were assumed to contribute to the rent and other more minor changes. At each cut, large numbers of recipients had their benefit reduced and, in total, 1.4 million households lost benefit rights altogether.[31] The majority were pensioners, but families with children have also been among the losers.

In parliament in 1985, the government made it clear that it would 'be looking to housing benefits to make significant reductions in the social security budget'.[32] Until its own backbenchers exerted some pressure for improvements, the government was prepared to see a further 110,000 families with children lose benefit outright in 1988.[33] Perhaps the most telling figure was the government's estimate that only 100,000 families on family credit — that is, less than a quarter — would also receive housing benefit after April 1988.[34]

While some may argue that the housing benefit scheme is an exception because of the size of the bill involved, they should remember that the social security budget is always under continuous pressure. Once the new family credit scheme is well established and its total cost is known, it would be a bold prophet who would predict that it will have no critics or that government will not one day — perhaps sooner than expected — see in it the potential for cuts to reduce public expenditure.

Does a fully means-tested system work well?
It could also be argued that too much is being made of recent experience and that, in other circumstances, means-tested benefits would be seen to be better for the poor. But is this really so in the long term? References are sometimes made to the social security arrangements in Australia, where virtually all benefits are means-tested or asset-tested or both. This is an example of a social security system in an advanced country targeted on low income people. However, an inspection of the model in action shows persistently low benefits below Australia's own poverty line — which is agreed to be austere. In the words of one Australian social security commentator:[35]

> Contrary to the argument that selectivity makes the best use of limited resources, the truth is that selectivity actually makes sure that welfare resources remain limited.

The point is that, when benefits (or services) are restricted to people on low incomes, the standards set cease to be those applicable to the rest of society, but become those considered sufficient for poor people. The service offered will usually be poorer and the incomes of poor people will be compared with one another's and with those who are only marginally better off (the near poor), not with those prevailing in the rest of society. The benefits of improved national prosperity will not be passed on to poor people, but they will be expected to take a major share in any economic cuts that are deemed necessary. This is usually done by claiming that money is going to people who are not 'really poor' or to people who are only a little worse off than many who are not entitled to help. Because the poor have been separated off in this way, there can be little protest about these actions from the wider public who are unaware of the true situation. Instead of a sense of national unity, in which *all* share the benefits of improvements in the national standard of living and *all* take their *fair* share of harder times, we have a divided nation, bringing with it all the disadvantages it implies for the whole country. But this need not be the case. As the ILO states in its publication, *Into the Twenty-first Century: The Development of Social Security*, we can have a more unified nation by keeping or implementing universal benefits which 'contribute to a nation's sense of community and inter-dependence — to national solidarity'.[36]

So, in the long run, isolating the poor from the rest of society is detrimental for everyone. The poor are better served by benefits in which all families have an interest (of which child benefit is an example), and which promote the integration of low income people into the wider society. Just as the National Health Service is supported by the majority of the population, both because everyone is concerned about the quality of a service they may need for themselves and because they take a pride in the fact that all children are entitled to equally good treatment, so also we find that the majority of families with children (eighty per cent) support child benefit[37] for their own needs and for the benefit of all families, and are critical of its being undermined.

Several references have been made in this chapter to the advantages of increases in child benefit. But before discussing whether these could be financed, it is necessary to look at the case for and against paying child benefit to families who cannot be regarded as poor. In the process, some of the other functions of child benefit will be examined.

Notes
1. Institute of Directors, *The Welfare State (1), Submission to the Review of Benefits for Children and Young People*, London, July 1984.
2. *Hansard*, 20 October 1986, cols 244-8.
3. Department of Health and Social Security, *Social Assistance: A Review of the Supplementary Benefit Scheme in Great Britain*, DHSS, London, 1978, p 38.
4. Green Paper, *Reform of Social Security*, Vol 1, Cmnd 9517, HMSO, London, 1985, pp 12-13.
5. Green Paper, *Reform of Social Security*, Vol 2, Cmnd 9518, HMSO, London, 1985, p 20.
6. As note 4 above, p 14.
7. Green Paper, *Reform of Social Security*, Vol 3, Cmnd 9519, HMSO, London, 1985, p 20.
8. *Hansard*, 17 December 1984, cols 49-50.
9. *Hansard*, 27 July 1979, cols 557-8.
10. *Hansard*, 27 October 1987, col 180.
11. As note 10 above, col 181.
12. As note 5 above, p 48.
13. Alan Hedges and Jenny Hyatt, *Attitudes of Beneficiaries to Child Benefit and Benefits for Young People*, SCPR, London, 1985, p 36.
14. *Mother's Life-line: a survey of how women use and value child benefit*, CPAG, 1985.
15. Anne Corden, *Taking up a means-tested benefit: the process of claiming Family Income Supplement*, HMSO, London, 1983.
16. National Association of Citizens Advice Bureaux, *Housing Benefit — the Cost to the Claimant*, NACAB, London, 1984.
17. John Major, interviewed by Richard Berthoud, in *Poverty*, CPAG, Spring 1987.
18. *Hansard*, 10 November 1970, cols 228 and 230.
19. *Hansard*, 12 November 1987, col 609.
20. *Hansard*, 9 June 1986, col 85.
21. Dilnot and others, *The Reform of Social Security*, IFS/Clarendon Press, Oxford, 1984.
22. Association of Independent Businessess, *Response to the Green Paper, 'Reform of Social Security'*, September 1985.
23. White Paper, *Reform of Social Security*, 1985, Cmnd 9691, p 32, on the subject of family credit.
24. *First Report of the Social Security Advisory Committee*, HMSO, London, 1982, p 32.
25. Association of Directors of Social Services, *Response to the Green Paper on Reform of Social Security*, 1985.

26 Frank Field MP, *The Guardian*, July 1984.
27 Nicholas Scott MP, Minister for Social Security, *Hansard*, 9 Nov 1987, col 85.
28 Sir Brandon Rhys Williams MP, *The Times*, 26 September 1987.
29 *Hansard*, 30 October 1987, col 65.
30 As note 11 above.
31 Dominic Byrne, 'The Great Housing Benefit Robbery', *Low Pay Review*, Low Pay Unit, Spring 1987.
32 *Hansard*, 3 June 1985, col 41.
33 *Hansard*, 14 February 1986, col 603.
34 *Hansard*, 16 November 1987, col 442.
35 Francis Castles, 'Trapped in an Historical Cul-de-sac: The Prospects for Welfare Reform in Australia', in Peter Saunders and Adam Jamrozik (eds), *Social Welfare in the late 1980s: Reform, Progress or Retreat*, Sydney, 1987, p 97.
36 ILO, *Into the Twenty-first Century: The Development of Social Security*, Geneva, 1984.
37 As note 7 above, p 83.

3 Child benefit, tax and the family

The fact is that child benefit provides the only recognition in the tax or benefit systems of the extra costs of having children. This is a good principle. We would be alone amongst almost all the countries of western Europe if we turned our back on child benefit.
Norman Fowler, when Secretary of State for Social Services[1]

This statement by the government offers some recognition of the way in which child benefit functions as a tax relief. Many of those members of parliament and others who deplore the payment of child benefit to families who are not poor prefer to ignore its tax relief function. To them it is simply and solely a social security benefit and, as such, should be reserved for the poor alone.

There are others opposed to universal child benefit who do acknowledge that it could be seen in part as a tax relief, but who argue that parents have children from *choice*, and therefore have no right to expect special treatment relieving them of the duty to pay the same tax as others who have made different choices.

A third view accepts that child benefit is a form of tax relief, but argues that, beyond a certain level of income, it can reasonably be withdrawn. The debate here is about where the line should be drawn.

What these three points of view have in common is a desire to withhold child benefit from high income families. What is the point, the argument goes, of paying a social security benefit to, for example, duchesses and people whose children attend Eton or Benenden?[2] There are other groups who wish to see child benefit paid only to those too poor to pay tax but who want to see child tax allowances restored for families with children.[3] These groups want to differentiate between a direct cash payment — even if it is in the form of a tax credit — and the additional income that arises from a reduction in the liability to pay tax. Moreover, some would like to see strict limits placed on increases in the cash payment, but would seek the maximum reduction in tax liability — even though the limits would be placed on extra income to low income people, while the greater increases in income through tax reductions go to middle and high income groups. The point will be taken up again in Chapter 7 where the public expenditure versus tax cuts argument will be discussed more fully.

Is child benefit a form of tax relief?

Before 1977, there were two ways in which families with children received financial support. The first of these was instituted in 1909, when child tax allowances were given to some (and later all) families with children. Its objective was to ease the tax burden on those who had the extra cost of supporting children, and so increase their take-home pay.[4]

Nearly 40 years later, the second form of help was introduced — the family allowance. This covered all children — except the first — rich or poor; but, since it was decided at the time not to withdraw the child tax allowances, family allowance was made taxable.

By the early 1970s, there was what was widely agreed to be a thoroughly unsatisfactory situation. Families too poor to pay tax got no benefit from the child tax allowance and, if they had only one child, no family allowance either. Indeed, the family allowance was so low that it gave larger families very little help anyway. Those who did pay tax got help with all their children, including the first, but the child tax allowance was worth much more to those with incomes high enough to pay higher rates of tax than it was to the ordinary family on the standard tax rate. It was true that richer people paid the higher tax rate on the family allowance; but this did not remove their advantage, because the benefit was so low.

To get out of this mess, and to give more help to poor families, both political parties developed plans for combining the family allowance and the child tax allowance into a child tax credit. The Conservative government got in first with a proposed tax credit scheme which would include a child tax credit. Originally it was to have been paid through the father's wage packet, but this idea aroused such a storm of opposition from women (who would be losing their family allowance) that it had to be abandoned. Instead, a universal child credit was to be paid for all children, including the first, direct to the mother by order book at the post office. But before this could be introduced, the government fell.

The Labour government which followed dropped the main tax credit scheme — which had presented many difficulties — but pursued the child credit plan. It did this by introducing child benefit in an Act passed in 1975. This allowed for the phasing out of child tax allowances, and the joining together of the resources thus saved with the expenditure on family allowance, to meet the costs of a new combined child benefit. Fathers lost their child tax allowance and mothers gained an improved child allowance. In the parlance of the time, the money was transferred 'from the wallet to the purse'. The measure received support from all sides of parliament and the Conservatives made a point of claiming credit for the idea.[5]

But politicians forget

When the decision was made in 1973 to pay a universal child credit direct to the mother, the Tax Credit Study Group — made up of senior civil servants from the Inland Revenue and the DHSS — pointed to a possible danger. The child credits, they said, 'are in the first place credits against income tax...they are a form of tax relief'. But, the Group went on to say, if they were paid to all mothers, they could lose the appearance of a tax relief:[6]

> People might then in time come to argue, on the one hand, that child credits should be subject to tax (as are family allowances at present) or, on the other hand, or possibly at the same time, that a separate allowance in respect of children should be given for income tax purposes.

It was a sound prophecy. The Conservative leadership, while in opposition, made every effort to hold on to the idea that child benefit was a personal tax allowance in a different form:

> Conservative aims in opposition were to secure 'an improvement in the real value of child benefit as part of an overall reduction in the burden of taxation.'
> Press Notice, July 1977

> Further improvements in child benefit would form part of our plans for increased personal tax allowances.
> Private Office of the Prime Minister, in a letter to CPAG in May 1979

Once the Conservatives were well established in government, little more was heard about this. Indeed, one of the government's early actions was to refuse to uprate child benefit in the November 1979 social security upratings. But the Inland Revenue has continued to regard the benefit as a form of tax relief. Because child tax allowances were withdrawn, the ordinary tax figures showed that the tax threshold for families with children had fallen — that is, families came into tax at a lower level of income. To set the record straight, the Inland Revenue calculated what it called a 'tax break-even point'. Because child benefit was not taxed, it formed a band of tax-free income. It should therefore be treated as a tax credit. If this was done, a 'tax allowance' could be calculated which would show the true level of the tax threshold. In a 1982 example (given by the Treasury) child benefit at £5.85 per week was equivalent, at the thirty per cent rate of tax, to a child tax allowance of £1,014 per annum.[7]

What is a tax relief for?

The case for regarding child benefit as a form of tax allowance (or a tax relief) for those liable for tax is, therefore, well-founded and leading backbench Conservatives have not lost sight of this:

> Child benefit should go to everybody. That is why it is a good benefit. It is said that it costs £4.6 billion... but this is an accounting fallacy because it is largely a tax allowance.[8]

The following statements from the National Federation of Women's Institutes and the Conservative Women's National Committee respectively show that it is an important issue for women's groups too:

> Child benefit is regarded as acting effectively as a tax allowance. For this reason members would like to see child benefit retained in its present form. Its value should not be eroded as its recent uprating for November appears to threaten.[9]

> The Committee feels that [an increase in child benefit] would be entirely appropriate, remembering that child benefit has replaced the former system of tax allowances.[10]

But what are the various kinds of tax relief expected to do? First, they limit the impact of income tax. By giving personal allowances, government can avoid taxing the poorest. If these allowances are allowed to fall behind inflation, or if they are set too low in the first place, individuals and families will be brought into the tax net, even though they cannot afford to pay tax. The provision known as the Rooker-Wise-Lawson amendment (after the Labour and Conservative MPs who proposed it) requires the government to index the personal allowances in line with inflation. Government policy in recent years has in fact been to increase the personal allowances by significantly more than inflation. Unfortunately, neither of these policies has been applied to child benefit.

A second function of tax reliefs is to achieve greater fairness in the distribution of the tax burden. Given an equal income, the ability to pay tax (the taxable capacity) is lower for people with children than it is for childless people. A tax allowance — or a child credit — is a way of putting those with and without children on an equal footing. (The technical term for this is 'horizontal equity'.)

To withdraw child benefit from non-poor families, or to allow it to fall in value, would be to abolish or weaken this element of fairness.

Tax reliefs have a third function. They can be intended to encourage, or to avoid discouraging, certain expenditure choices which the government regards as desirable. Governments have, for example, wanted to encourage home ownership and private pensions. Taxpayers who opt for these receive tax relief on a large part of the expenditure. The fact that these are free choices does not disqualify the person from tax relief. On these grounds, there should be no reason to deny tax relief to parents who *choose* to have children. The giving of tax relief for children was intended to ease the economic burden of parenthood and thus to avoid discouraging people from child-bearing — though it was never set so high as to constitute an incentive to have children. In the context of tax reliefs in general, this was a perfectly proper decision.

The great majority of tax reliefs that an individual can claim do not distinguish between lower and higher incomes. Whether on a low or high income, each individual who earns enough to pay tax can claim the personal allowances, or mortgage interest tax relief or pension relief. The maximum amount of tax relief is the same for all. But this does not produce an equal outcome for all earners. The tax allowances are worth more to high earners who pay the higher rate of tax than to lower earners who pay the standard tax rate. This is because for each £1 that is taxable, high earners pay 40 pence in tax but lower earners pay 25 pence. Therefore, when that £1 is taken out of tax, the higher earner gets more benefit out of the change. In addition, although most men (though fewer women) earn enough to claim their personal allowances, higher earners are in a better position to spend money on some items which are eligible for tax relief — for example, a private pension.

Child benefit as a tax relief offers a much fairer deal. It does not achieve absolute equity. What it does do is to offer the same amount of tax-free income for each child. It could be argued that this band of tax-free income is worth more in taxes saved to the higher rate taxpayer than to the standard rate family — though the gap has narrowed significantly in recent years. But paying child benefit as a child tax credit, rather than as a child tax allowance, offers important advantages over other forms of tax relief. Child benefit ensures that every family receives its maximum entitlement — unlike pension tax reliefs, for example. As a flat-rate benefit, it provides a higher proportion of both family income and expenditure on the child for low income families than for high income families. And it goes direct to the caring parent — which, government-sponsored surveys show, means that it is spent directly or indirectly on children in the overwhelming majority of cases.[11]

The treatment of child benefit

How has this tax credit been treated since 1979? In the period 1979 to the present date, the government has frequently stated its objective to reduce the tax burden. To this end, the single person's personal allowance has risen nineteen per cent ahead of the rate of inflation, and the married man's allowance by twenty-two per cent. By 1987, child benefit was already three per cent below its 1979 value, and the decision made in April 1988 to freeze it means a reduction in its real value by another four per cent. Arguing the case against freezing child benefit, Sir Brandon Rhys Williams MP said:

> The decision to freeze child benefit was incompatible with the policies for which the Prime Minister has won widespread approval -- namely her support for the family as an institution, and her desire to reduce the tax burden on families and to encourage the British people to work and save for their independence.[12]

In fact, child benefit has ceased to be treated as a tax allowance (or relief). It is now classed as social security expenditure and, as such, the government would like it to be either held down or, if possible, cut. Consequently, families with children are not being given their full share of the benefit of tax cuts through higher tax allowances — a share that would, no doubt, have been available to them had the old discredited child tax allowance still been in existence.

Should the rich be given child benefit?

At its present level, child benefit as a tax credit cannot really be regarded as excessive, even for the rich. There is a temptation to suggest that one would not be in a hurry to go to the stake to preserve tax reliefs for the children of the richest families in our society. Just the same, we need to be cautious before throwing the rich overboard.

First, there are relatively few rich families with children -- the supply of duchesses is quite limited and so are parents of Eton boys and Benenden girls. In the mid-1980s, only four and a half per cent of parents paid tax at the higher rates — these figures are unlikely to have changed to any great extent.[13] But the example of these families has been used to make a case for changing the nature of child benefit altogether.[14] This could have adverse effects on the other ninety-five and a half per cent who are not rich.

Second, the expenditure savings gained by withdrawal of child benefit from the rich would be comparatively small. The likelihood is that the government, once started on this type of policy, would go on to draw the cut-off line lower and lower. Again, many more families than the rich would suffer.

Third, child benefit is the only recognition given to the extra costs that all families with children carry in comparison with those who are childless. If it is withdrawn from people on higher incomes, there will almost certainly be pressure to restore child tax allowances which, as seen, produces unfair results relative to the flat-rate child benefit. Indeed, it is quite likely that giving child tax allowance to higher earners would be more expensive in revenue terms than the child benefit which was withdrawn — an absurd outcome.

If a way could be found to exclude rich families without these adverse effects, all well and good. But if it cannot, then it may be better to accommodate the rich minority in the present scheme — to which they have some rights in tax relief terms — in order to preserve the interests of other families. But should any non-poor families get child benefit? It is to this question we turn in the next chapter.

Notes

1. *Hansard*, 18 June 1985, col 159.
2. *Hansard*, 27 October 1987, col 185.
3. Institute of Directors, *Submission to the Review of Benefits for Children and Young People*, 1984.
4. *Hansard*, 2 September 1909, col 508.
5. *Hansard*, 13 May 1975, col 342.
6. *Minutes of Evidence to the Select Committee on Tax Credit*, 15 February 1973, 64-v, HMSO, London, 1973, p 72.
7. Evidence by HM Treasury to the Treasury and Civil Service Subcommittee on *The Structure of Personal Income Taxation and Income Support*, 12 May 1982, HC-331-iv, HMSO, London, 1982, p 208.
8. Sir Ian Gilmour MP, *Hansard*, 12 November 1987, col 619.
9. National Federation of Women's Institutes' response to the Social Security Green Paper, September 1985.
10. Conservative Women's National Committee, Pre-Budget Submission, 1984.
11. Benefit Payments Report on a survey about *Methods of Payment for Child Benefit and Retirement Pension*. Prepared for the Department of Health and Social Security by the English Market Research Bureau Limited, London, October 1985, p 23.
12. Sir Brandon Rhys Williams MP, *Hansard*, 27 October 1987, col 186.
13. Richard Berthoud and John Ermisch, *Reshaping Benefits: the Political Arithmetic*, PSI, London, 1985, pp 97-98.
14. Dilnot and others, *The Reform of Social Security*, IFS/Clarendon Press, Oxford, 1984, p 116.

4 Child benefit for all families – sharing the cost of children

So far we have considered the poor and the rich. However, the majority of families lie between these two extremes. For them, child benefit has acted in two ways — as a tax relief and as a social benefit through which the cost of child-rearing is shared by the community.

No need to help non-poor families?
While it is fairly easy to take up a clear-cut position on the payment of child benefit to the rich, the large group of middle income families presents more problems to those who are questioning the present child benefit arrangements.

The case for sharing the costs of children, set down by Beveridge in the 1940s,[1] is now seen by some as outdated. At that time, the social norm was that women would give up (paid) work when they married or when they had their first child, and they would return to work — if at all — when the children were over school-leaving age. In that period also, families were often larger on average than they are today. In 1951, for example, nine per cent of married women had five children or more, including eighteen per cent of women married to unskilled manual workers and fourteen per cent of those married to other manual workers.[2] Nowadays, it is commonly accepted that married women will go out to work. Large families are now a tiny minority in Great Britain and, though they are still common in Northern Ireland,[3] the typical UK family now has one or two children.

What is argued from this is that women are able to return to the labour force without serious hindrance. If the family needs additional money to support the children, the remedy is in its own hands. While full-time work may not be practicable, opportunities for part-time work are expanding and are expected to do so for some time to come.[4]

The fact that women can earn is also seen to dispose of another argument for maintaining child benefit in its present form. Its opponents say that if child benefit is essential to women because it provides one of the few, and often the only, source of income over which women have control and which they can use in the best interests of the children, then, since women can earn through work, they can provide their own source of independent income. Again, the case for universal child benefit is seen as outdated.

It is acknowledged that a scheme to assist low-earning families is essential; but this is said to be the function of the new family credit scheme. If it is desired to help families who could be classed as near poor, this scheme can be allowed to reach higher up the low income scale beyond those who are really very poor. Indeed, it is already planned to do this to some extent.

Not all of those who wish to end the universal payment of child benefit would restrict help to the poor or even the poor *and* the near poor. They acknowledge that some families a bit higher up the income scale could appropriately be given help with the costs of children. Some have proposed that the line be drawn at the level of two-thirds of the average income. Others have suggested setting the cut-off point at average income or higher still. Child benefit could thus be either withdrawn or replaced once a certain income was reached.[5] But no clear plan for limiting child benefit in this way has yet emerged — at least not for public scrutiny.

Finally, some hold the view that it is right to retain child benefit as a universal benefit so as to give some recognition to the costs of child-rearing and to express a general community concern for families. But this role of child benefit will not necessarily rate a very high priority in the allocation of resources.

If it is deemed desirable to give more to poor families, then non-poor families can expect to have to stand back and see part of their benefits — or an expected benefit increase — transferred to those in real need. In any case, where families are not in need, a few pence here or there will make little difference to them. This was the argument used by Nicholas Scott, Minister for Social Security, to defend the freeze in child benefit in 1988:[6]

> Child benefit is, and will remain, a valuable contribution to the extra costs that every family incurs as a result of bringing up children...and the purpose will continue to be met whether the benefit remains at £7.25 or goes up by 30p.

The universal benefit as a form of tax relief

A notable feature of this line of argument is its failure to recognise that child benefit also acts as a form of tax relief, intended to ensure fairness between those with and those without children. In 1987, eighty-five per cent of families who received child benefit were taxpayers.[7] The case for tax equity for middle income families is clear, and would almost certainly not be under question if this tax relief were still given in the form of a tax allowance.

According to figures given in *Hansard* for 1986, around 1.4 million children lived in families with total household incomes near or above twice the average income.[8] About half of these could be classified as rich and the rest quite comfortably off. But, as observed in Chapter 3, even this group could be seen as reasonably entitled to a modest tax relief for the children.

The great majority of children — over 8 million — live in families whose household incomes range from well below the average income through to twice the average income. All of these families have a right to some recognition in the tax system for the cost of child dependants. They could also reasonably expect that the tax relief they do receive — child benefit — would be increased in line with other personal allowances. In the words of Sir Brandon Rhys Williams MP:[9]

> Cutting down the real value of child benefit, or cutting it out altogether, narrows or eliminates the differential between families with children and families without them. I do not see why that differential should cease to exist for people who are better off.

The cost of a modern child

There is one difference between 1945 and 1988 which is pointed out less frequently by those who say that child benefit is out of date. The *demands* on the family budget for children's needs are higher now than they were then.

Studies about the minimum costs of children by David Piachaud, commissioned by the Child Poverty Action Group,[10] suggested rates which were widely accepted as realistic, though some might think them rather austere — see Fig 8.

Age	Piachaud's rates (£ per week)
2	11.40
5	13.00
8	15.70
11	16.60
13-15	30.10

(House of Commons Library, Research Note on Child Benefit, 9 November 1987)

Fig 8 — The minimum costs of children, September 1987

The figures in Fig 8 (in which Piachaud's estimates have been updated to September 1987) show the estimated minimum cost of a child — and the word 'minimum' should be emphasised. Parents interviewed in a DHSS-sponsored study published in 1985 spoke of the high cost of a newborn baby, new pressures on the family budget when a child starts school and the very high demands when the child reaches secondary school age. One mother described some of the pressures she faced:

> First year of their secondary school when they come home, 'I've got to have a geometry set, I've got to have my own set of coloured pencils, I've got to have this, that and the other.' That's not even on the school uniform list. And you've got another £10-15 on top of the bill you've just spent to rig them out with all the school uniform.[11]

The high cost of supporting a child through the education system has also increased because the school-leaving age has been raised twice since 1945, extending the years of dependency. The move into a more technological age, the lower demand for unskilled labour, the need to relate to a European economy and other similar factors all create demands not only on the education system throughout the school years, but on the parental budget as well. Demands also stem from the examination system and the increasing stress on qualifications. The government constantly emphasises the importance of seeing that children are fully equipped for the modern labour force. It is worth noting also that, in 1983, there were 913,000 families receiving child benefit for at least one child aged 16 years or over.[12] Parents like these are bearing particularly heavy costs for a very expensive age group — 16 and 17 year olds. Even with child benefit it is hard to meet the demands:

> But even from the school, a day in France, £14, I think, for the day — how can you say 'No, you can't go'? Plus they have to have packed lunch and spending money. She had a history thing for her O levels or whatever it is, and she had to visit three old houses. I had to pay £5, now that's only to further her education. If she didn't go she couldn't write her essays and she couldn't do her examination.[13]

A child must not only be clothed and educated. S/he must also be fed, housed and kept warm in winter. All of these carry a price tag; and in the case of housing and fuel, the costs in recent years have increased well ahead of the rate of inflation. Some mothers are only just managing to cope:

> With the rising costs of mortgage payments and the cost of heating fuels, my child benefit means we are just keeping our heads above water. Without it we would sink.[14]

Bringing up a child is not only a matter of physical care. The parent has to prepare the child to live in the wider society outside the family. The child must be introduced to a variety of social roles and relationships, through play, collaborative social activities, etc. These also carry monetary costs.

These demands on the family suggest that, far from freezing or abolishing child benefit, there could well be a case for increasing it so that the community's share of the cost of children reflects modern realities and expectations of the family. The amount each family spends on its children varies a great deal, but what they have in common is that, if they are to do their best for their children and meet the demands the government and the community make of them, this will involve considerable expenditure.

Women and employment

It is true that the period that women spend out of the labour force has declined, on average, to around eight years.[15] But this general statement needs more detailed examination.

With a child aged 0-4 years:
  75% remain at home
  19% work part-time
  6% work full-time

With a child aged 5-9 years:
  44% remain at home
  43% work part-time
  13% work full-time

With a child aged 10-15 years:
  31% remain at home
  45% work part-time
  24% work full-time

(*General Household Survey*, HMSO, 1983 — for Great Britain)

Fig 9 — Married women, children and paid employment

Recent surveys show that eighty-eight per cent of women go out to work in the period between marriage and the birth of their first child, and a proportion of the remainder would have been pregnant at the time of marriage and worked until then.[16] Thereafter the figure drops sharply, as Fig 9 shows. It is important to note from this that a significant proportion of women are at home caring for children, though in declining numbers as the children grow older.

Women with more than one child, and especially those with larger families, are more likely to stay at home to look after their children.[17] This is particularly the case for women in Northern Ireland. Another common reason for women to stay at home is the lack of affordable day-care provision for the under-fives and after-school and holiday care for the over-fives. Some women are kept out of the labour force by the need to care for a handicapped child or an adult relative who needs constant attention. Some women may, of course, choose not to be in paid employment because financially there is no need for them to be.

> If we want parents to do a decent job, let us start by recognising that responsibility has a price tag. Depressing living standards at a time when there is often only one income is a nonsense.
> Sir George Young, Conservative MP
> *The Guardian*, 20 November 1987

Figures produced as a result of any one survey taken at a particular time never give the full picture. Women, typically, cease employment at the time their first baby is born and stay at home caring for the child while s/he is very young. They may then return to work, usually in a part-time capacity, but may give up work again when a second child is born. Once that child is old enough, and if it is the last, a more regular work pattern can develop.

But many women's part-time jobs are in the service industry and may be seasonal. In addition, for the labour market the value of married women, particularly part-timers, is that they form a labour 'reserve' which can be taken on and laid off according to market needs. Married women who have been earning enough to pay national insurance contributions may have unemployment benefit to tide them over periods of unemployment; but the very low paid group will not, and will have no rights to other benefits of their own.

The wages earned by those who do work will not usually be high. As Fig 2 (page 8) shows, the vast majority of part-time women workers and half of all those working full-time fall into the low paid category. Moreover, going out to work involves further expenditure; the cost of a childminder for the children, for example. Some families can arrange their hours of work so that either the husband or wife is at home to care for the children. Others may not be able to do this, and do not have relatives who will oblige; so the cost of day care comes high. One mother of three wrote to the Child Poverty Action Group earlier this year:

> If child benefit were taken away I would have to go out to work and put my children in nursery care, the only problem being that in Gloucestershire we have no government-run day-care services so I would have to find £30-40 per week per child and I would have two little ones to pay for.

The Equal Opportunities Commission have also emphasised the need to maintain child benefit for women in particular:[18]

> The decision to retain universal child benefit is welcomed but

this will only be meaningful in the long term if a commitment is also made to maintaining its real value... Child benefit assists family income at a time when the mother's earnings are nil or substantially reduced. When mothers return to work, child benefit assists families to meet child-care costs.

Women also incur many hidden costs. A recent study has suggested that a typical mother who gives up work for several years to stay at home looking after her children forgoes up to £122,000 over her work lifetime. These lost earnings result, first, from her period of withdrawal from the labour force; second, because she must limit her hours of work in order to meet her family commitments; and third, because she loses experience and career opportunities and cannot therefore command the wage rates that would otherwise have been available to her.[19]

Women bear these losses as part of their parental responsibilities. These responsibilities may mean missing out on promising employment opportunities in the interests of the children. It is therefore not surprising that many women are angered at proposals to abolish child benefit and feel a sense of hurt that the community — or, more correctly, some vocal individuals and at times the government — seem to place such a low value on the task of child-rearing.

Women's work and family income

The growth in the participation of women in the labour market is an important development, but needs to be seen in a wider context. It is of much greater advantage to the childless family, or to one where the children have grown up, than it is to a family with dependent children. Where there are no children, there can be two full-time earners — or a part-time job can be selected for its wage level rather than its location and hours which would enable it to be combined with child-rearing. Moreover, a simple comparison between the incomes of households with and without children does not tell the full story, because it takes no account of the number of people dependent on that income. When the Child Poverty Action Group carried out a survey in 1984, one mother said:

> I know I am not poor, but the fact remains that I have to work in order to supplement family income. Child benefit is an essential part of our total income and we do depend on it.

Richard Berthoud of the Policy Studies Institute made an analysis of the incomes of non-pensioners, using the Family Expenditure Survey. He included women's earnings and assumed, for simplicity's sake, that everyone claimed all the benefits to which they were entitled. He called their total the 'final income'. He calculated the minimum needs of the family based on the then long-term rate of supplementary benefit and a fixed housing allowance, but allowed the children the equivalent of a long-term benefit rate — which they do not now receive.[20] His chart, shown here, makes very clear the differences between households with and without children. Households with children are bunched at the lower end of the income distribution. Two-thirds of families with children have a standard of living below the national average, while two-thirds of other adults are above the national average.[21] Again, the figures suggest a need to increase, not decrease, child benefit.

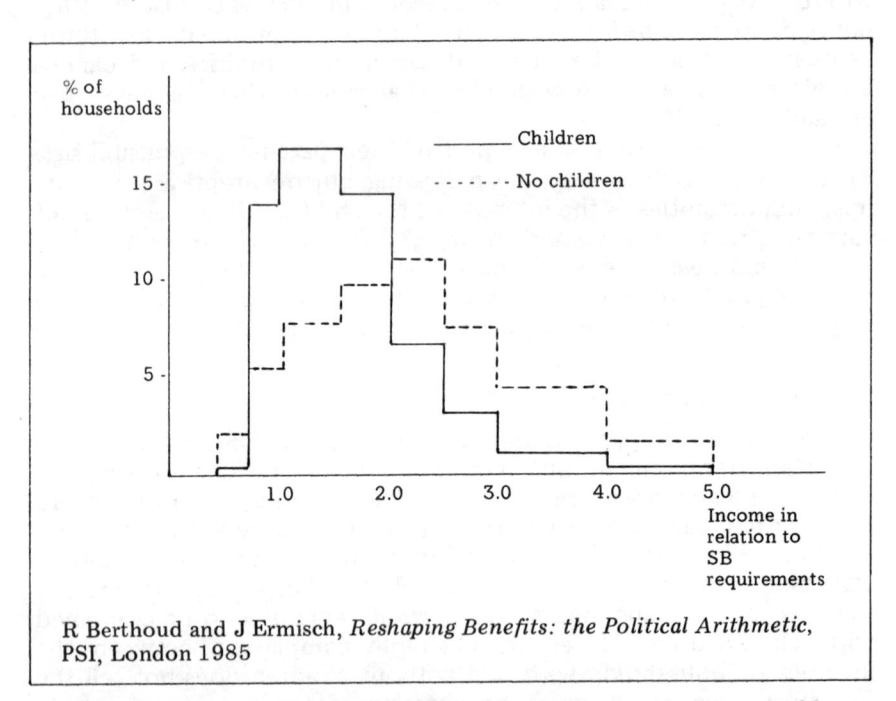

R Berthoud and J Ermisch, *Reshaping Benefits: the Political Arithmetic*, PSI, London 1985

Distribution of income in relation to requirements: households with and without children

Child benefit and families with modest incomes

As seen earlier, those who seek a much more restricted child benefit argue that the new family credit scheme will go sufficiently far up the low income scale to assist the near poor with children. As long as this is done, they argue, child benefit for other families can be downgraded.

Families with two young children earning up to £140 per week in wages will receive some family credit, and those with older children would receive some help on earnings of up to £160 per week. Housing benefit, on the other hand, would cut out at earnings around £100 per week in wages for new claimants.

So, in the immediate future, family credit will help those who are just non-poor, especially those with older children whose costs are highest. But the history of housing benefit (as set out in Chapter 2), and its present rates, do not inspire confidence that family credit will always be available to this income group. Even if it did, the cut-off point is well below the average wage. Bearing in mind the high cost of children, and especially of older children, families well above the 'near poor' level will still need child benefit.

> We are an ordinary average family, lucky enough to own a house and be employed. We don't live extravagantly, and often have a job to make ends meet — we certainly couldn't manage without family allowance.[22]

> I know there is also an argument that well-off families shouldn't get the benefit, but the problem is where to draw the line. We are just the wrong side of the line usually drawn for any help, and certainly wouldn't want to do without child benefit, indeed we would find it very difficult.[23]

Spreading the load

The period during which parents are bringing up their children is usually the time of highest financial demands. Not only must the costs of the children be met while one potential earner is out of the labour market or restricted in hours or choice of employment, but a home must be established and built up. Parents have to look to their own future too — through pension contributions and provision against loss of earning ability, including the death of a partner.

Help is available with the purchase of a house — through mortgage interest tax relief — and this is given regardless of income, whether or not there are children, and with little long-term cash return for the public who are footing the bill. Pensions and other similar provisions are also given tax relief — though in this case there will be some return to the public, since the pensions, once payable, will be taxed.

Child benefit, as a means of spreading the load, probably offers the best future returns. The children, as adults, will themselves become taxpayers, helping to support future generations of children as well as the elderly, and making their contribution to the national economy. The better the job the parents have been able to do in bringing them up, the better the contribution the children will make to the public well-being in the future — and not only in financial terms. By sharing the cost of children at the time it is needed, the community is not only showing that it values children and the parental role — it is making a shrewd long-term investment.

Notes
1 Social Insurance and Allied Services (the *Beveridge Report*), Cmnd 6404, HMSO, London, 1942, pp 154-8 and 49-50.
2 Elizabeth Overton, *Recent Changes in Fertility in Great Britain*, CSSP, London, 1977, p 84.
3 *Social Security Statistics, Great Britain and Northern Ireland*, HMSO, 1984.
4 Manpower Services Commission, *Corporate Plan 1986-1990*, MSC, Sheffield, 1986.
5 For example, see *Hansard*, 30 January 1984, col 112; 27 March 1984, col 168; and 2 April 1984, col 365.
6 Nicholas Scott MP, Minister for Social Security, *Hansard*, 12 November 1987, col 608.
7 *Hansard*, 22 October 1987, col 480.
8 *Hansard*, 25 July 1986, col 668.
9 Sir Brandon Rhys Williams MP, *Hansard*, 2 November 1987, col 93.
10 David Piachaud, *The Cost of a Child*, CPAG, 1979; and *Children and Poverty*, CPAG, 1981.
11 Alan Hedges and Jenny Hyatt, *Attitudes of Beneficiaries to Child Benefit and Benefits for Young People*, SCPR, London, 1985.
12 *Hansard*, 16 July 1985, col 120.
13 See note 11 above.
14 Mother of two, *Mother's Life-line: a survey of how women use and value child benefit*, CPAG, 1985.
15 Jean Martin and Ceridwen Roberts, *Women and Employment: a Lifetime Perspective*, Department of Employment/OPCS, HMSO, London, 1984, p 21.
16 See note 15 above, p 125.
17 General Household Survey, HMSO, 1983.
18 *Reform of Social Security: Response of the Equal Opportunities Commission*, August 1985.
19 Heather Joshi, *The Cash Opportunity Cost of Child Bearing: an approach to estimation using British data*, CEPR, London, 1987, pp i-iii.
20 R Berthoud and J Ermisch, *Reshaping Benefits: the Political Arithmetic* (previously published as *Changing Family Benefits: Aims and Outcomes*), PSI, 1985, pp 55-6.
21 R Berthoud, PSI research briefing, *Welfare: Mixing the Sheep and the Goats*, 1987.
22 Mother, as note 14 above.
23 Mother, as note 14 above.

5 The protection of children

The functions of child benefit discussed so far are the principal reasons for its existence; but child benefit has proved to have valuable characteristics which exceed the expectations of those who first set out to introduce this benefit. Some people argue that these added advantages are merely useful bonuses which can be abandoned if they get in the way of reform. But there is a better case that argues that child benefit is particularly well placed to respond to modern realities and that the added advantages should be welcomed and, if possible, reinforced.

Changes in family circumstances

The first of these added advantages comes into play when a family undergoes a period of instability, in the make-up of the family, for example, and/or in the level or regularity of its income. In times of difficulty such as these, child benefit payments continue, protecting the interests of the child. Whether sympathy or blame is accorded to the parents for the difficulties they find themselves in, the child is *always* the innocent party. A benefit which recognises this fact is, therefore, to be valued.

It is worth noting that child benefit has acquired this function not so much because *it* has changed — though the inclusion of the first child after 1977 was an important development — but because *society* has changed. Not surprisingly, it was not thought necessary in 1945 to give family allowances the task of providing against family instability, since it was not then such an urgent problem. However, the signs that were showing up in the 1970s, when child benefit was introduced, are now clear, and for the foreseeable future there seems no likelihood of a return to earlier patterns.

Marriage breakdown

It has always been the case that a proportion of marriages have ended in separation and, when available, divorce. Where there were children, they experienced the change from being part of a two-parent home to one with a lone parent only — a change which had both social and financial consequences.

Year	No. of divorces
1950	38,900
1970	71,660
1985	160,000
1986	154,000

☐ In 1986, 56% of all divorcing parents had children under 16 years old — 151,964 children in all

☐ 1 child in 5 could see their parents divorced before they reach 16 years of age

(*Finer Report*, Cmnd 5269, and *Family Policy Studies Centre Bulletin*, Autumn 1985 and Winter 1987/88)

Fig 10 — Divorces in England and Wales

Early figures for the number of separations are hard to come by, but the numbers of separated mothers who required means-tested support suggest that in 1950 they were still a small minority.[1] Divorce statistics are, however, available and the figures in Fig 10 show the large increase which has taken place in recent years. The pattern in England and Wales is replicated in Scotland and, to a lesser extent, in Northern Ireland.

Most of these families will have gone through a period of financial upheaval. The income of the parent left caring for the children will probably have been irregular — while agreements were being hammered out or court orders awaited — and it will almost always have been considerably reduced.[2] It may remain irregular even when all the processes have been gone through. The only reliable income, paid week in, week out, may well be child benefit. It provides an island of stability in a sea of uncertainty and protects the child against the worst effects of this financial stress. One woman described the financial insecurity that can follow separation or divorce:[3]

> I am a single parent, not on social security because officially my husband supports us, but he is very casual about his support. I cannot guarantee a weekly contribution from him so for weeks on end I rely on child benefit.

Re-marriage and re-divorce
The child's circumstances can change again through the re-marriage of the caring parent, and yet again if the new marriage ends in divorce.

> Re-marriages after divorce or widowhood:
> 1971   21% of all marriages
> 1986   37% of all marriages
> Divorces where one or both parties were previously divorced:
> 1972   9% of all divorces
> 1985   23% of all divorces
>
> (England and Wales — *Family Policy Studies Centre Bulletin*, Winter 1986/87 and 1987/88)

Fig 11

In these cases, where there are children, sometimes the natural father will be supporting the child, sometimes the stepfather, sometimes a working mother and sometimes nobody at all, except perhaps through means-tested assistance. Again, the one stable element will be child benefit, which will follow the child through this maze, via the caring parent.

Births outside marriage
In the 1950s, four per cent of births were to parents not married to each other. By 1986, this had risen to twenty-one per cent of births; but two-thirds of these were registered by both parents and the assumption was that they were living together.[4] In the 1950s, cohabitation was relatively uncommon. By 1985, it had become commonplace and, indeed, has shown a sizeable increase since 1979.[5]

The parents of children born to these unions may marry each other; but they may separate and marry other partners. Again, the financial circumstances of the caring parent will fluctuate and once more child benefit will help to protect the child:

> I urge the Minister to recognise the merits of child benefit, especially its ability to provide stability despite the fluctuating circumstances of the family and the protection that it provides to children by providing a measure of independent finance for the mother.
>
> Ronnie Fearn MP, 1987[6]

Unemployment
Changes in the level and regularity of income do not occur only through marriage and divorce. Another prime cause of financial instability is unemployment. The relevant figures here are not so much the numbers who are unemployed at any one time, or even the length of unemployment — though these are prime causes of child poverty. In terms of economic instability, it is, rather, the number of

people who are newly unemployed for a period during the year. It is not easy to find an accurate figure; but a good indicator is the number of claims for unemployment benefit. These have increased significantly over the last few years, and have doubled since 1950.

Year	No. of claims
1950	2.7 million
1965	2.4 million
1971	2.9 million
1978	3.6 million
1980	4.1 million
1985	5.4 million

(Ministry of Pensions and National Insurance, *Annual Reports* and *Social Security Statistics*, HMSO, London)

Fig 12 — Number of claims for unemployment benefit

These figures represent those who lost their jobs once in the year and soon returned to work; those out of work once and still unemployed at the end of the year; and those who have had several spells of unemployment during the year. These figures include both men and women. (It should also be remembered that many unemployed married women do not appear in these figures because they had no entitlement to unemployment benefit.)

Where there are children, the loss of the work income of whoever is the main family breadwinner must have a serious impact. DHSS figures from a survey of unemployed people showed that, even with benefits for unemployment, the income of the majority of men (usually the main wage-earners) dropped by half.[7] The loss of the job of the second earner (usually the wife) will not always have such a serious impact, but in many families it is these earnings which keep the family out of poverty or near poverty. During these periods, when income is reduced, often severely so, child benefit plays its stabilising role on behalf of the children. Two women, taking part in a survey in 1987, described how crucial child benefit was at times of financial insecurity caused by unemployment:

> [Child benefit is] at present a secure source of income for mothers and children in a very insecure employment market.[8]

> It's the only bit of financial help when a woman stops working and is not able to claim unemployment benefit.[9]

What does the future hold?
All the forecasts tell us that high unemployment is likely to be with

us until the end of the century, albeit at a lower level than that of recent years. What is more, the nature of the labour market is changing. Whereas in the past long-term stability was the norm, in the future labour market flexibility will be the key requirement. Marginal and insecure forms of employment are likely to expand. Fewer jobs will be permanent. Firms responding to the market will lay off workers when they do not need them and take them (or some of them) on again if and when they do. More jobs will be subcontracted and more people will be self-employed. There will be more seasonal work in the growing service industries.[10]

Such a future prospect means that, though there may be fewer people unemployed at one time, there will be larger numbers who experience a period of unemployment and/or fluctuations in their income during the year. Indeed, this is implicit in the government's hoped-for enterprise society. To succeed, there must be a willingness to experiment with different forms of work, to move from declining to growing industries, to take risks by setting up in business as a self-employed person, to be willing to be re-trained even at a temporary income loss, and so on. All of this means that the child's need of protection in times of income instability will be greater, not less.

Similarly, there is no reason to expect that attitudes to marriage and divorce which have grown up in recent decades will alter to any great extent in the future. Indeed, in 1984, the government made divorce a little easier by reducing the length of time after a marriage when divorce proceedings can be initiated.

All of this suggests that child benefit will be much needed in the future — so much so that some family organisations have argued that it should be increased to the point where the child is 'endowed' with an income which will guarantee it the minimum needed for its support. Certainly, any decision to increase the benefit would strengthen its ability to protect children in times of change. As Conservative MP Virginia Bottomley argued in 1987:[11]

> People's domestic situations change, their income changes with longer or shorter hours and their accommodation changes. Therefore child benefit provides the stability that is required.

The most obvious casualties of economic instability are low income families, because they have so few reserves. But families at all income levels break up and, whatever the income before the split, the caring mother (in particular) may well be left with little or nothing until a settlement is reached. Families who are better off can more easily survive unemployment, but can also be brought low by it.

There are, of course, benefit provisions which support families through periods of family change or unemployment. But for the child these have limitations and deficiencies. There may be delays in decisions about benefit eligibility. In addition, many benefits have rules attached to them which may be relevant for adult behaviour but have nothing to do with the children. Benefits may be reduced because it is judged that the adult concerned is out of work through his/her own fault. A decision to re-marry or cohabit means the loss of one-parent benefit (a small benefit payable per family, regardless of the number of children), perhaps before the responsibility for child support has been settled.

For families whose income fluctuates a good deal — because they are in and out of work in the most insecure sector of the labour market, or because they are subject to periods of illness or perhaps are disabled and struggling to keep a place in the labour market — the benefit provisions present particular problems. The benefit administration cannot cope with these frequent changes, so payments lag behind needs. Other benefits (family credit, for example), are based on the giving of 'rough justice' and do not attempt to match the benefit with the time of need too closely.

In the light of all this, it is clear that child benefit could not fulfil its function to protect the child if it were means-tested. The key to its usefulness is its universality. It is available when the crisis occurs — not many weeks later, when the mother has discovered that she might be entitled to it and has finally proved her eligibility. It is not affected by rules intended for adults, or subject to delays or withdrawals or reductions. It is there, in payment, and will continue to be so throughout the period of insecurity and beyond.

Child benefit and one-parent families

In 1945, when family allowances were being legislated, one-parent families were still a small minority who rated little priority in policy making.[12] The figures in Fig 13 make it clear that this group can no longer be so easily disregarded. Nor can the 1.6 million children in these families.

☐ In 1984 there were 940,000 one-parent families
☐ 87% are headed by a woman; 13% by a man
☐ Children in one-parent families — 1.6 million
☐ One child in every eight lives in a one-parent family

(*Population Trends*, Autumn 1986, and *Family Policy Studies Centre Bulletin*, Autumn 1985 and Winter 1987/8)

Fig 13 — One-parent families — Great Britain in 1984

Government figures for 1983 showed that four-fifths (780,000) of one-parent families fell within the low income band. These families always have a very high rate of dependence on means-tested benefits — it has been estimated that seventy-three per cent of them could qualify under the new schemes.[13] Inevitably, their standard of living is low.

The route to a higher income and ultimate self-support is most likely to be through paid employment. But it is a long, hard road. Hours of work often have to be limited because of family commitments; the wages of women are low; and the unemployment and poverty traps are inevitable accompaniments of the means-tested benefits they need.

Two elements of their benefit income are not means-tested — child benefit and one-parent benefit. They are the stable base on which a better standard of living can be built, because they do not fall as income rises. Child benefit is particularly important where there is more than one child.

Any increase in child benefit would assist lone parents to achieve self-support, free of means-tested benefits. Its continued payment, after a slightly higher standard of living has been attained, provides a valuable element of reliability and stability in families where, for example, time may be lost from work because the child is ill or because day-care arrangements have broken down.

The benefit has another advantage. It is sometimes suggested that one-parent families are given more favourable treatment than two-parent families, and that this ought to be reversed. Whichever way it is looked at, a policy of increasing other benefits for lone parents at the expense of child benefit does not necessarily help one-parent families, and certainly disadvantages two-parent families. Child benefit, on the other hand, is paid equally to all types of family. Any upgrading of the benefit is of advantage to all, two-parent and one-parent families alike.

Income-sharing within families

The third advantage that universal child benefit offers is that it helps to protect the interests of children in families where the income is distributed unfairly between its members. There is growing evidence that in some families, apparently quite affluent ones, the husband reserves much of the income to himself, does not pass wage rises to his family and takes little note of inflation in the allowance he makes to them.[14] In addition, he may expect to be asked for his permission for any spending, so that he maintains his control. One woman described the added pressures a situation like this created for her:[15]

> Ronald didn't like me buying anything for the children. If I went out and bought them a pair of shoes and he wasn't with me, there was hell to pay when I got home. He just didn't like me

spending any money without his consent. If he wanted to go out and buy things that was different. He was keen on photography and bought a lot of photographic equipment. What things he needed to buy were OK...

Not all fathers act in this way, thankfully, and many recognise the need to share the income:

Even as a man, I recognise that not all husbands give their wives enough provision for their children.[16]

If, in situations like these, the marriage finally breaks down, the mother may find herself (or at least may feel) better off, even on the low income provided by social security:

I'm better off, I think. Although I have less money, it's all mine to allocate where I want. It's made a difference to how I organise money because I have control now.[17]

Another woman, while receiving less actual income, felt herself to be in a stronger position:[18]

I'm worse off overall. I probably have less money... But I feel as though I'm better off.

Mothers in families such as these particularly value child benefit because it is paid direct to them and they can use it to provide for the children's needs.

Some commentators (usually male) tend to dismiss this issue as relatively unimportant, or at least not to see it as a matter for government concern. Michael Beenstock suggested in 1985 that miserly husbands might reduce the wife's housekeeping money by all or some of the child benefit she receives. He added: 'Most probably the issue is not sufficiently important to be a major constraint on reform...'[19] The Institute for Fiscal Studies (IFS) — which was recommending that allowances for children should be paid through the husband's pay packet — suggested that what happened within the family was a private matter and that 'the forced redistribution of considerable amounts of money from husband to wife might be resented by many people, including the authors of this book'.[20]

The government should, however, expect considerable resentment from women if it contributes further to the poor distribution of money in many families by paying child benefit through the father's wage packet (as it seemed to be considering in the Social Security Green Paper);[21] and it *did* experience much hostility when it tried to pay family credit in this way and had to withdraw this proposal. And this hostility is unlikely to be restricted to women suffering hidden poverty. In most families it is the mother who has to juggle the family finances to see that the children's needs are met.

It is probably fair to say that a government should not be expected to introduce child benefit with the object of protecting children from poverty hidden within the family. But, since child benefit exists and *is* serving this purpose, this factor can and surely should be taken into account in making decisions for future policy.

Paying child benefit to the mother

The IFS proposal that benefits for children be paid through the father's pay packet raises another issue — the usefulness of the present method of payment from the point of view of the child.

Women do value the way child benefit is paid, because it gives them a source of independent income which thay can spend in the interests of the children, and, as seen in Chapter 3, child benefit is spent on the children in an overwhelming majority of cases. Organisations concerned for the well-being of children also know from their experience that by paying the benefit direct to the caring parent — usually the mother — there can be much greater confidence that the children will be given priority in the spending of the benefit:

> Because child benefit is generally paid directly to mothers, it constitutes the most effective source of security for children. Experience has shown that in times of hardship, money paid to the mother will almost invariably go to children first.[22]

Others think money should be 'earmarked' for children, as is child benefit, rather than have it form part of a general family benefit. As the British Association of Social Workers argued:[23]

> Even if the total income of the family were not increased through child benefit owing to interaction with taxation, the value of payment through the primary carer would persist and it would earmark a minimum sum that each family should devote to the support of the children.

The payment of the benefit to the mother was a principle fought for in 1945 and again when the tax credit proposals were being made.[24] Many believe it to be an important principle in the interests of future children, including the Conservative Women's National Committee:[25]

> We strongly urge you not to overlook the significance of child benefit being paid directly to the mother...

Notes

1 Joan Brown, *In Search of a Policy: the rationale for social security provision for one-parent families*, NCOPF, London, 1988, pp 28-9.
2 The Law Commission, *Family Law: the financial consequences of divorce*, HC68, HMSO, London, 1982.

3 Mother in Cambridge, child benefit survey, 1987.
4 *Social Trends.* HMSO, 1988.
5 See note 4 above.
6 Ronnie Fearn MP, *Hansard*, 12 November 1987, col 626.
7 Sue Moylen and others, *For Richer, For Poorer?*, DHSS Cohort Study of Unemployed Men, HMSO, London, 1984, p 96.
8 See note 3 above.
9 Mother, child benefit survey, 1987.
10 MSC, *Corporate Plan, 1986-90.*
11 *Hansard*, 2 November 1987, col 699.
12 See note 1 above, pp 45-6.
13 John Haskey, 'One-Parent Families in Great Britain', *Population Trends*, Autumn 1986.
14 Richard Berthoud, *The Examination of Social Security*, PSI, London, 1985, p 85.
15 Mother, in Melanie Henwood and others, *Inside the Family*, Family Policy Studies Centre, 1987.
16 Father, child benefit survey, 1987.
17 See note 13 above.
18 See note 13 above.
19 Quoted in *Hansard*, 1 March 1985, col 602.
20 Dilnot and others, *The Reform of Social Security*, IFS/Clarendon Press, Oxford, 1984, p 110.
21 Green Paper, *Reform of Social Security*, Vol 2, Cmnd 9518, HMSO, London, 1985, p 48.
22 National Children's Bureau, *Evidence to the Review of Benefits for Children and Young People*, 1984.
23 British Association of Social Workers in evidence to the Social Security Review, 1985.
24 Joan Brown, *Children in Social Security*, PSI, London, 1984, pp 37 and 61.
25 Conservative Women's National Committee, Pre-Budget submission, 1985.

6 Changing the nature of child benefit – the consequences

The size of the annual bill for child benefit makes it a constant focus of attention. Some want to see it abolished completely. Others would means-test or tax it. Others would freeze it at its present level. Some would be content just to withdraw it from the rich; others want to restrict it to the poor. There are different views, too, on how the money saved should be used. It could provide better means-tested schemes for the poor, or a higher child benefit for those who did get it. It could instead — or in part — be used for tax cuts, or go into the general pool of revenue available to the government.

Until recently, governments were prepared to go on the record in support of child benefit as a universal benefit of considerable importance to families. The present government gave what appeared to be a firm endorsement of the present child benefit in its 1987 election manifesto. However, there are now plenty of signs that the government is seriously considering a major change in child benefit, which could substantially reduce its effectiveness or remove it altogether.

In examining the possibility that the nature of child benefit will be changed, it is necessary to ask two questions. The first is, what will be the principal consequences for families of the various ways that could be chosen to cut child benefit? The second is, what effect, good or bad, will the proposals for redistribution of the savings have on families? This chapter will deal with the first question. The next chapter will consider the second.

Abolishing child benefit

Until recently, it would never have been thought necessary to discuss the possibility of abolition. No government had put it forward as a serious proposition; and this government, in 1986, categorically rejected it:[1]

> He may regard what I am going to say as the 'same old tripe' from the Government Front Bench, but we believe that universal child benefit is desirable. We are likely to be boringly consistent on that point for the foreseeable future and, I hope, permanently.

But now there are more doubts about the future of the benefit; so it is necessary to analyse the effects abolition would have:

- ☐ It would deprive all families of the tax relief which takes account of the fact that they have children to support.
- ☐ It would remove the help given to families with modest incomes and so reduce their ability to give their children a good start in life.
- ☐ It would bring at least another half a million families, with one million children, into the net of means-tested benefits.
- ☐ It would deepen the poverty trap because the whole of the benefits which supplement low wages would be subject to deductions of 80 pence or more for each extra net £1 earned through additional effort.
- ☐ It would reduce the number of people who can make the leap from unemployment to full self-support, without the need to claim means-tested benefits or being caught in the poverty trap.
- ☐ It would reduce the security of families seriously affected by economic or family stress or both.
- ☐ It would signal to the country that a low value is placed on children and on family life in comparison with other objectives of public expenditure or with the aim of reduced expenditure.
- ☐ It would leave the UK as the only country in Europe in which there was no provision for the ordinary family in the tax/benefit system for the costs of bringing up children.

Freezing child benefit

This is a favoured choice of governments because it is the easy option. It was used almost as a normal policy in the treatment of family allowances between 1946 and 1974. During that time, family allowances were increased only four times, including two increases in 1968. The result was a drastic decline in the value of the benefit,[2] which contributed to the need for major reform in the 1970s.

Since child benefit was introduced, families with children have had a higher priority; but child benefit was still frozen in November 1979, increased below the rate of inflation in 1985 and frozen again in 1988. The difference between the two periods, however, is that child benefit now has wide-ranging support which crosses political party lines *and* class and income lines. As a result, a policy of freezing cannot be pursued without adverse political consequences. The freeze in one year has, therefore, usually been reversed in the next; so that while the value of child benefit has fallen since 1979, the fall, until April 1988, was limited to three per cent in real terms.

But there is now a new element in the situation. The 1988 freeze was justified on the grounds that it released resources which could be devoted to low income families. In other words, families are being put in competition with one another for help with the costs of children.

It seems possible now that a policy of freezing on a regular basis could again be adopted. It may even be seen as a route to eventual abolition.

This last point is not a fanciful idea. There are a number of precedents. Benefits which have been frozen for a long time have been abolished since 1980 on the grounds that their value was so low that they were not worth paying. These include the maternity grant, the death grant, the injury benefit and the industrial death benefit, as well as several other minor benefits. The Liberal Party, recognising precisely this danger, made the following statement in 1985:[3]

> The Liberal Party believes in the need for a universal index linked child benefit, paid to the caring parent. We would oppose any moves to allow it to decline in value every year until it is regarded as being so low it is not worth keeping and costs too much to maintain.

While any gradual decline in the value of child benefit takes place through a policy of freezing, it will have a number of consequences:

☐ It will reduce the value of the band of tax-free income given by child benefit and thus increase the impact of taxation on all families with children.
☐ It will limit, more and more each year, the help given to families on modest incomes, to whom the benefit has been important in their efforts to do the best for their children.
☐ It will have a particularly severe impact on large families — especially in Northern Ireland, where larger families (both Protestant and Catholic) are still common.
☐ It will offer less and less help and security to those experiencing family or economic crises.
☐ It will gradually force more and more families, who have been able to maintain their independence, to apply for means-tested benefits.
☐ It will weaken, year by year, the springboard provided by child benefit which enables people to move from unemployment to full self-support.
☐ It will slowly but surely intensify the poverty trap.

In any one year it will still be possible to say 'what difference does a few pence really make?'. But the cumulative effects of a year by year decline in the value of child benefit will be felt by all the families in this country. As the Northern Ireland Assembly pointed out, it makes a significant difference, especially to larger families:[4]

> [Government failure to uprate child benefit in line with inflation] raises the regrettable possibility that even if the basis of child benefit is not to be changed, its value may continue to diminish. In Northern Ireland, where average family size is

greater than in Great Britain, such a development would have especially damaging consequences.

Means-testing child benefit

The possibility of means-testing the benefit is another regular suggestion. It was examined and rejected in the Social Security Review, as Norman Fowler himself explained:[5]

> The government believe that the extra responsibilities carried by all those bringing up children should be recognised. Child benefit will, therefore, continue to be paid for all children, irrespective of the means of the parents.

Means-testing, as it has been proposed in the past, does not necessarily mean restricting the benefit to the very poorest (though that is the goal of some). The problem that arises with means-testing is where to draw the line:

☐ If the benefit was available only to the poorest, the fact that it was means-tested would mean the loss of all those advantages which child benefit currently offers in relation to the unemployment and poverty traps and in its avoidance of take-up problems. (These have been spelled out at length in Chapter 2 and will not be repeated here.)

☐ Unless a benefit, set at a reasonable level, was paid to families in the middle income ranges, the goal of assisting families with the costs of children would be abandoned. Given the importance these families place on the universal child benefit, this would be seen as a rejection of the value of the family and the parental role.

☐ If the means-test line was drawn so as to include the non-poor, and operated so as to reduce child benefit progressively as income rose, there would, in the words of a government minister (Tony Newton), 'be considerable extra administration costs arising from the need to subject seven million families receiving child benefit to an incomes test'.[6] It would also raise the difficulty of means-testing millions of fathers for a benefit paid to mothers.

☐ Again, it must be remembered that child benefit is equivalent to a tax credit or allowance. Means-testing a tax allowance is rarely done. The only example within the personal allowances is the age allowance. However, this is an addition to the ordinary personal allowance for the elderly on low incomes. Its removal as income rises has no effect on personal allowances — for married or single people — which, far from being means-tested, have recently been increased across the board in real terms. It is these allowances which are the equivalent in the tax system to child benefit for children.

☐ If the objective of means-testing is to reduce the cost of child benefit so as to facilitate tax cuts, then the effect would be to redistribute, in part, to single and childless people, resources now targeted on children.

For reasons such as these, the Scottish Convention of Women wrote:[7]

> We recommend that there should be no means-testing of child benefit. The concentration of resources on the very poor would be at the expense of those who are only marginally less poor... and not of the childless or those who have benefited from child benefit in the past.

Taxing child benefit

It will be recalled from Chapter 3 that an official committee in the 1970s prophesied that once family allowance and child tax allowance were integrated into a cash benefit — a child credit — there would soon be calls to tax the benefit. It was not many years before they were proved right.

At first sight, taxing the benefit would seem one of the more attractive options. It would recoup approximately £1.25 billion[8] and thus be a significant saving. Some of those proposing taxation see it as a more subtle way than most to introduce selectivity, without the disadvantages of means-testing. The principle of a universal benefit would be maintained, but part or even all of it would be withdrawn through taxation from those not considered to need it or all of it.

The objective of some is a simple reduction of social security expenditure. Others would like to see the savings gained from cutting child benefit expenditure used for tax cuts. A different objective is to find money to increase child benefit — the money saved in taxing it would be recycled, so as to increase the benefit for those on low incomes and give more help to those on modest incomes.

But the taxation of child benefit would produce both disadvantages and a crop of absurdities:

☐ To tax child benefit is to tax what is, in effect, a tax relief — an absurd situation in its own right.
☐ Even if this were not the case, the effect of taxing child benefit would be to increase the tax burden on families with children. For much of the last two decades, the distribution of the tax burden has been unfairly weighted against families.[9] There has been some (modest) improvement in this situation in recent years for some families — in which child benefit has played a part. It would seem foolish to move to reinforce the disadvantage of families through the taxation of a benefit paid only to those with children.
☐ At the present level of child benefit, which offers only limited tax relief for children, there is not even a particularly strong case for

withdrawing it from rich families, who are often the main target. If there was a desire to do this, the taxation of the benefit could be restricted to those paying the higher rate of tax; but only a tiny minority of parents pay above the standard rate. The tax take would therefore be quite limited. If there is a wish to tax those on higher earnings more heavily, there are better and simpler ways of doing this which do not single out families with children. In fact, the policy of the government has been to reduce higher tax rates, so that there is now only a single one, of forty per cent.

☐ If the benefit were made taxable at all income levels, then it has to be borne in mind that about eighty per cent of parents pay tax at the standard rate — including the near poor, those on modest incomes and those who are reasonably comfortably off. All of these would suffer the same reduction in income through the payment of tax at the going rate on their child benefit.

☐ Taxing child benefit would normally mean taxing the father on the benefit the mother was drawing. This could well bring about a call for the return of child tax allowances, with all the inequalities these involve (see Chapter 3 on this).

☐ An alternative suggestion has been to count the benefit as the mother's income. Quite apart from the fact that the revenue this would raise would be very limited, this could mean that, except for women who have their own unearned income, the tax would be paid by working mothers, not non-working mothers. But working mothers include many in low to modest income families who have gone out to work in order to keep, or remove, their families from poverty and/or to give their children improved chances in life. And non-working mothers include those whose family income is high enough to remove the necessity to work.

☐ Taxing the benefit in order to recycle the money in higher child benefit, while attractive, also has problems in the present tax system. The increase would flow through to all standard rate taxpayers to the same extent and be taxed back to the same extent. Non-taxpayers, the majority of whom are on means-tested benefits,[10] would only benefit if government policy on the treatment of child benefit and the child dependency additions were changed. In addition, although it is in fact a no-cost device for improving child benefit, it would produce the appearance of a large increase in public expenditure on higher benefits. Before long, the savings made through taxation would be conveniently forgotten and we would hear calls for reducing this 'expensive' benefit once again.

Taxation of child benefit, if not an outright reduction of public expenditure by cutting the income of families, will do one of two things. First, it could redistribute money, which was directed to families, to *all* taxpayers (that is, assuming the money is used for general tax cuts); or, second, it could place on families alone the cost of supporting, through recycling, the cost of improving benefits for other families. The closer one examines the taxation option, the more dubious it seems:

> The great majority of working families pay tax so that the effect would be equivalent to a thirty per cent reduction in child support. Put another way, for a family with two children the effect would be the same as reducing their tax threshold by about £700 a year. The government's aim is to take people out of tax, not bring them into tax.[11]

Notes

1. John Major MP, when Minister for Social Security, *Hansard*, Standing Committee B, 6 March 1986, col 684.
2. Joan Brown, *Children in Social Security*, PSI, 1984, p 56.
3. Liberal Party's response to the Social Security Green Paper, 1985.
4. Northern Ireland Assembly, *Report on the Green Paper on the Reform of Social Security*, 1985.
5. Norman Fowler MP, when Secretary of State for Social Services, *Hansard*, 13 June 1985, col 35.
6. *Hansard*, 21 November 1985, col 286.
7. Scottish Convention of Women in evidence to the Social Security Review, March 1984.
8. *Hansard*, 27 June 1985, col 481.
9. See note 2 above, p 112.
10. R Berthoud and J Ermisch, *Reshaping Benefits: the Political Arithmetic*, PSI, 1985, p 97.
11. Green Paper, *Reform of Social Security*, Vol 2, Cmnd 9518, HMSO, London, 1985, para 4.35, p 47.

7 Allocating resources wisely

Governments, of course, have a duty to 'husband' the nation's resources and see that they are spent wisely — including the money spent on child benefit. But this does not mean people should automatically assume that cutting child benefit is the right option. This should only be done if there is a sound case for doing so, *and* if it can be ensured that such a cut to the benefit will not have damaging effects. As this pamphlet has shown, neither of these has yet been established.

Until a couple of years ago, it seemed that the only way to achieve an increase in child benefit was to 'find' money within the current tax/benefits system that had not been wisely allocated and to shift it to child benefit. But more recently, additional resources have been made available to allow for substantial tax cuts. This raises the question of whether these resources might be better used. But, before discussing these two ways of funding an increase in child benefit, two matters have to be got out of the way.

Counting the cost — a mental blockage

The first of these is the way in which expenditure is treated by the government and the Treasury. As Hermione Parker (research assistant to the Conservative MP, Sir Brandon Rhys Williams) wrote in *The Times* (4 June 1985):

> At a time when millions of people are both taxpayers and beneficiaries the old concepts no longer make sense. The Treasury's antique accounting methods which count cash benefits as public expenditure (and therefore bad) and tax relief as negative income (and therefore good) are not only absurd but dangerous. It is because of this convention that child benefit is a prime target for cuts...

In recent years, there has been much discussion about 'modernising' social security through integrating it more closely with the tax system. The Conservative government's tax credit proposals of the 1970s, and the introduction of child benefit from 1977, were seen as examples of such modernisation. A tax allowance would be converted into a cash benefit — a child credit — but would still be treated on the same basis as the other personal tax allowances. But the problem was — and is — that the old-fashioned accounting methods operated by the Treasury cannot cope with the more modern approach to tax relief that child benefit represents; and there is no sign that the government has recognised the need to change these methods, in spite of its frequent references to the need not to be tied down by blind adherence to the past. Sir Ian Gilmour (a Conservative back-bench MP) pointed to some of the flaws in the government's attitude when he said:[1]

> We all know that there are two sides to a balance sheet. Not paying in on one side is exactly the same as taking money out on the other side.

To the Treasury (and the present government), personal allowances are revenue not collected, while child benefit is public expenditure on social security. From 1978/79 to 1986/87, the cost of child benefit increased by £2.7 billion,[2] mainly to keep it in line with inflation. In the same period, reductions in the tax rate, increases in personal allowances and other tax changes reduced the 'tax take' by £9.5 billion, offset by £1.4 billion gained by abolishing the twenty-five per cent reduced rate tax band.[3] The increase in the cost of the child tax credit — child benefit — is regarded by the government as a cause for alarm and a reason for considering policy change. The money allocated to tax reductions is seen as a cause for self-congratulation by the same government.

If we could once clear this mental blockage by which we are being trapped in the past (when tax credits were an unknown quantity), it would be possible to examine rationally the way in which the resources available should best be allocated.

The targeting of child benefit

> I have no specific proposals at present to change the nature of child benefit, but . . . in view of its cost and ill-targeted nature there is clearly a need to keep it constantly under review.

John Moore MP, Secretary of State, in his statement above,[4] uses the word 'targeted' as a means of describing benefits which are concentrated on low income people. But whether a benefit is well- or ill-targeted depends on what its target is. The target for child benefit is families with children, not poor families. If its wide-ranging functions can each be justified — and this pamphlet has argued that they can — then it is well-targeted.

There may still be a case for keeping it under review, because of social change, but the case for restricting it to a small proportion of families has not been established. What is more, when the benefit was subjected to intensive scrutiny in the Social Security Review 1984/85, the government reached the same conclusion:[5]

> Child benefit is designed to meet the needs of families generally. ...The case for changing it has not been made out.

One of the unusual features of child benefit is that, although it is expected to perform a wide variety of functions, these are compatible with one another. In this pamphlet, it has been shown that each of these functions is weakened if child benefit is weakened. It is equally true that each of them can be strengthened if child benefit is strengthened.

Can we afford an increased child benefit?

Since 1979, there has been a drive to cut public expenditure as one of the means by which the economy could be improved. Whether or not this is a right or effective policy, the fact is that the government now has substantial sums of money available to it with which it can exercise choices.

In spite of this, social security ministers continue to refer to the money available for allocation to social security as 'rare resources'[6] and to suggest that 'extra help is not available to go to the most needy because resources that could otherwise go to them are tied up elsewhere'[7] — ie, in maintaining universal child benefit.

But there *is* money available, which could go to families with children. There is no real dispute about this. Indeed, the media commonly refer to the Chancellor of the Exchequer's coffers as being 'awash' with money. Today's debate is not about whether there is money to spend, but about how best several billions of pounds should be used.

The married man's tax allowance

Under the present system of personal allowances, a married man receives an allowance worth approximately one and a half times a single person's allowance, on the grounds that he has a dependent wife to support. If his wife works, he does not lose this additional allowance. He keeps it and his working wife gains an entitlement to the equivalent of a single person's allowance as well, so that the married couple enjoy total allowances worth two and a half times that of a single person.

In 1980, the government issued a Green Paper, *The Taxation of Husband and Wife*.[8] It wished to review the married man's allowance in the light of the increased participation of women in the labour force. It also wished to remove another anomaly: the fact that the wife had no privacy in her tax affairs. Her income was treated as if it were her husband's for tax purposes, and all correspondence on her tax affairs was conducted with her husband and him alone.

One of the proposals urged upon the government by many organisations (including the Child Poverty Action Group) was that the money that would be saved by the abolition of the married man's allowance for those under pension age should be converted into a higher child benefit. This would target the money on families with children as the families in which the wife was most likely to be unable to work, or work full-time, and it would strengthen the tax relief for children. It would be an effective nil-cost method of increasing child benefit and would be in harmony with the original reason for giving the married man's allowance, that is, a recognition of the costs of supporting a dependant.

The government announced in the 1988 Budget that, as from 1990, husband and wife are to be taxed independently on all of their income. All taxpayers, married or single, male or female, will be entitled to the same personal allowance to set against their own tax liabilities. So far so good. *But* the government went on to say it will be providing an additional married couple's allowance, equal to the difference under the old system between the married man's allowance and the single allowance. This will go to the husband in the first instance, but he will be able to transfer any unused portion of it to his wife.

Almost everyone agrees that the resources being used on the present married man's allowance are badly targeted. Exactly the same can be said about the proposed married couple's allowance. It will benefit families with two full-time earners, and families with incomes so high that the wife can choose not to go out to work, even if she has no dependent children. It is true that it will also give some help to families with one earner and children, or in cases where the wife is limited to part-time work because of the demands of the children. But if the resources involved were instead converted into a higher child benefit, they could be wholly targeted on families with children and offer a boost to income where it is most needed.

The government, thus, has resources available to assist families in a practical way. But it is choosing instead to maintain the status quo as far as it can.

Tax reductions

The government has frequently been urged to abolish, to tax or means-test child benefit so that the money released could be used to cut taxes. The *Sunday Times* printed an editorial arguing this case:[9]

Child benefit, however, is the worst offender. This benefit, currently costing £4.5 billion a year, goes to millions of families who are not in real need. If it was drastically pruned to only those on the supplementary benefit line, it could yield £4 billion in savings. The child benefit cut alone would yield enough to allow a 3p cut in the standard rate of income tax. But some of the savings could also be used to assist those most in need by taking them out of tax altogether.

Most proposals of this type suggest that some of the money saved from child benefit would be redirected to those in need,[10] but they usually share with the *Sunday Times* and with the government[11] the assumption that tax cuts would be of benefit to low income families, and indeed to all families and, by implication, more beneficial or as good as an increase in child benefit. But is this really the case?

	Multiples of average earnings — 1986/87			
	¾ *average*	*average*	*twice average*	*5 times average*
	£	£	£	£
1p cut in basic rate	0.97	1.54	3.44	3.44
6% increase in personal allowances	1.23	1.23	1.69	2.54
5% increase in tax thresholds	1.00	1.00	3.08	9.25
£2 increase in child benefit	4.00	4.00	4.00	4.00
(*Hansard*, 16 March 1987, cols 385-6)				

Fig 14 — Increase in income after tax (£ per week), married man, 2 children

During 1985[12] and again in 1987,[13] the government was asked parliamentary questions as to the effect of allocating the same amount of money to various ways of cutting tax and to increasing child benefit. The 1987 example given by the government (shown in Fig 14) was on the effect of spending £1.3 billion on the four options shown. As can be seen, for a couple with two children, child benefit offered the greatest advantage in the majority of cases (the exception relating to a man on five times average earnings).

It is also argued that tax cuts which take lower income people out of tax or reduce their tax rate also act to reduce the poverty trap. This is correct; but child benefit has the same effect and is better targeted on families with children. Thus, from the point of view of families with children, the wisest use of that £1.3 billion would still have been an increase in child benefit. Since the government does

have the money available to allocate, it cannot be said that there is
no realistic opportunity for such an increase.

Although the government was well aware of these facts — indeed,
it produced the figures for parliament — it chose in its 1988 Budget
to allocate over £6 billion in the form of tax cuts through increased
personal allowances and reductions in the rate of tax. The cost of
reducing the higher rate of tax from sixty per cent to forty per cent
alone was over £2 billion.[14] At the same time, the intention to freeze
child benefit was maintained and the benefit itself was being attacked
as being badly targeted and going to families who had no need of
extra income.

A country without a child benefit

> The government accept the case for continuing the system of
> child benefit. It is right that families with children at all income
> levels should receive some recognition for the additional costs
> of bringing up children and that the tax/benefit system should
> allow for some general redistribution of resources from those
> without children to those who have the responsibility of caring
> for them.[15]

In making this statement in 1985, the government was in line with
the policy of governments throughout the European Community.
But there is one country, whose example we are often urged to
follow, which has no equivalent of child benefit — the United States.
What has their experience shown them?

The United States relies heavily on a means-tested benefit called
Aid to Families with Dependent Children (AFDC) to help poor
families. Studies, both official and independent, have shown that, in
the period 1973-84, the income of families with children has been
declining in real terms — most notably in low income families, but
also across the whole income range. A report in 1985 from the
Congressional Budget Office pointed out that households with children
now account for over two-thirds of all poor people in the US, even
though the proportion of children in the population has declined
over the past twenty years.[16]

Politicians and leading researchers are beginning to urge that the
US should introduce the equivalent of child benefit, referring to it as
a family allowance. Senator Moynihan, for example, has pointed out
that among the major democracies, the US is the only country without
a family allowance. He said that some people might call AFDC a
family allowance, but that this is typically paid to broken families.
He added: 'Why not a family allowance to support the traditional
family and help hold it together?'[17]

Similarly, a leading demographer has said: 'If we care about our collective future rather than simply our future as individuals we are faced with the question of how best to safeguard the human and material resources represented by children. These resources have not been carefully guarded in the past two decades,' particularly in the light of increasing marital instability. He went on:

> ...insisting that families alone care for the young would seem to be an evasion of collective responsibility rather than a conscious decision about the best way to provide for the future.[18]

Should child benefit survive?

The sheer range of criticisms made of child benefit in the past few years, first by some elements in our society and now by the government itself, creates the impression that there is a strong case for abolishing the benefit or at least cutting it, perhaps quite severely. Yet when each of the arguments against child benefit is subjected to rational examination, quite a different picture emerges. The case against child benefit has not been established, in spite of all the sound and fury.

On the contrary, the case *for* child benefit, and for an increased child benefit, emerges quite clearly and strongly from this detailed examination. Not only do all its acknowledged functions (as outlined in Chapter 1) remain valid and necessary, but a new and important function — child protection — has developed in recent years.

Nor has it been convincingly shown that the country cannot afford to invest in the family and in the future generation, through child benefit. The evidence that resources *are* available was placed clearly before us in the 1988 Budget. At the same time, moves to downgrade child benefit will most certainly have a seriously detrimental effect on all families.

The evidence presented in this pamphlet indicates how much the mothers of the nation's children value child benefit and how deeply they would resent its withdrawal or reduction. The message that families with children would receive would be that their task of child-rearing is not seen as worthy of the steady community support throughout the years of dependency that child benefit currently offers.

Child benefit is not a 'glamorous' benefit. It does not attract the headlines accorded to tax cuts. But in this benefit we have a good workhorse, which is able to serve a variety of purposes for the family and the country, and to serve them very well. There is no case for assigning it to the social security equivalent of the knacker's yard. Nor is there a case for weakening it through semi-starvation so that it can no longer do its work effectively.

There *is*, however, a case for making it stronger so that it can perform its tasks even better. There *is* a case for saying to families with children: 'We value you and what you are doing. We want to support you in your vital task, and we are more than willing to see resources invested in the future of the nation!'

Notes
1 Sir Ian Gilmour MP, *Hansard*, 12 November 1987, col 620.
2 Social Security Statistics; and *Hansard*, 27 October 1987, col 185.
3 *Hansard*, 10 February 1987, col 178.
4 John Moore MP, Secretary of State for Social Services, *Hansard*, 27 October 1987, col 186.
5 Green Paper, *Reform of Social Security*, Vol 2, Cmnd 9518, HMSO, London, 1985, p 47.
6 *Hansard*, 27 October 1987, col 186 (John Moore MP, Secretary of State for Social Services).
7 *Hansard*, 12 January 1988, col 208 (Nicholas Scott MP, Minister for Social Security).
8 Green Paper, *The Taxation of Husband and Wife*, Cmnd 8903, HMSO, London, 1980.
9 *Sunday Times*, 27 September 1987.
10 *Hansard*, 1 March 1985, cols 580 and 604, are examples.
11 *Hansard*, 10 April 1984, col 252.
12 *Hansard*, 15 January 1985, cols 117-8; and 3 December 1985, cols 173-4.
13 *Hansard*, 17 March 1987, cols 385-6.
14 *The Budget in Brief*, published by the Treasury, 15 March 1988, HMSO, London, 1988.
15 As note 5 above, p 48.
16 *Focus*, Spring 1986, p 6.
17 See note 16 above, p 10.
18 See note 16 above.

Now's the time to join CPAG!

We can help you . . . with the facts on poverty.
You can help us . . . in the fight against poverty.

CPAG membership gives you access to all the latest – on welfare rights, income inequalities, perspectives on policy, and lots more!

And CPAG members give us the support we need to ensure that poverty is at the heart of the agenda, whatever political party is in power.

Send off the form now, and join CPAG in working for a fairer future.

Please complete and send to: CPAG, 4th Floor, 1-5 Bath Street, London EC1V 9PY.

I would like to join CPAG as a comprehensive member .... (tick)
(Comprehensive members receive CPAG's regular journal, Poverty, plus welfare rights and social policy publications – for £30/year).

or I would like information about other membership options, ... (tick)

I enclose a cheque/PO (made out to CPAG) for £30 .... (tick)

Name _____

Organisation (if applicable) _____

Address _____

_____

_____ Postcode _____

A TAX ON ALL THE PEOPLE: THE POLL TAX
Carey Oppenheim

This simple guide puts the proposals to reform local government in political context. It offers a critical appraisal of how the poll tax will operate, its interaction with social security, and its impact on those who will suffer most

56pp   0 946744 06 8   Dec 1987   £1.95

Sent automatically to CPAG Comprehensive & Policy members

Please send me:

_____ copy/copies of *A Tax on all the People* @ £1.95 per copy (incl. p&p)

I enclose a cheque/p.o. for £ _____ , payable to CPAG Ltd.

Name _____

Address _____

_____

Town _____ P/Code _____

Return this coupon, with your remittance, to CPAG (Pubs), 1–5 Bath Street, London EC1V 9PY.

NEW CHILD POVERTY ACTION GROUP PUBLICATIONS

**Single Payments: The Disappearing Safety Net
edited by Ruth Cohen and Maryrose Tarpey**

Reveals the full impact upon claimants of the savage cuts made to the scheme in 1986. Evidence collected from CABx, local authorities, advice agencies and charities throughout the country shows a general level of hardship as yet largely ignored by the media and general public. Much of the evidence against the Social Fund is already here.

      96pp   Feb 1988   0 946744 07 6   £3.95

The Social Fund: What's Wrong With It?

A new 4-page A4 broadsheet detailing CPAG's basic objections to the scheme. Essential reading for anti-poverty campaigners.

      Feb 1988   65p

Please send me:

.... copy/copies of *Single Payments: the Disappearing Safety Net* at £3.95 per copy

.... copy/copies of the Social Fund broadsheet at 65p per copy

I enclose a cheque/p.o. for £ ...., payable to CPAG Ltd

Name ....

Address ....

Town .... P/Code ....

Return to CPAG Ltd, 1–5 Bath Street, London EC1V 9PY